On the Boundary

A Life Remembered

Fred Dallmayr

Hamilton Books

Lanham • Boulder • New York • Toronto • Plymouth, UK

Library of Congress Control Number: 2017942838
ISBN: 978-0-7618-6956-6 (pbk : alk. paper)—ISBN: 978-0-7618-6957-3 (electronic)

∞™ The paper used in this publication meets the minimum requirements of American National Standard for Information Sciences Permanence of Paper for Printed Library Materials, ANSI/NISO Z39.48-1992.

To all my students throughout the many years

One lives life twice: once in actuality, and once in memory. . . .
—Honoré de Balzac

The past is never dead. It's not even past.
—William Faulkner

Herkunft bleibt stets Zukunft.
—Martin Heidegger

Contents

Preface   ix

Acknowledgments   xi

On the Boundary: A Life Remembered   1
    Whose Life?   1
    Childhood: Augsburg   4
    School Years   8
    Legal Studies: Munich and Brussels   14
    Turin: European Institute   17
    To America and Back   20
    Return to America   23
    Purdue University   26
    The Two Cultures   30
    Political Theory and the Cold War   33
    Gadamer and Habermas   36
    Martin Heidegger   43
    Oxford and Postmodernism   46
    Notre Dame   54
    India: Beyond Orientalism   56
    Political and Continental Philosophy   61
    Multiculturalism and Globalization   64
    Dark Clouds: Wars Again   68
    In Search of the Good Life   72
    Democracy and Return to Nature   75
    Arab Spring, Russia, Asia   77
    Cosmopolitanism and New Horizons   82
    In the Darkness, Light a Candle   86

    A Preliminary Farewell   88
    Notes   89

Appendix A: "Sehnsucht Dorthin": A Response to Rasmussen and
    Flynn   103
    Note   112

Appendix B: Reason and Dialogue: My Road to Intercultural Studies   113
    Notes   118

Appendix C: Interview: Joseph Camilleri with Fred Dallmayr   119
    Note   124

Index   125

Preface

I had never intended to write an autobiography or a story of my life. To do so always seemed to me somewhat pretentious and a sign of undue self-preoccupation. After all, to "live" means to live among others or, in Martin Heidegger's words, to "be-in-the-world"—where world has multiple dimensions above and beyond the immediate environment. Moreover, I have been sufficiently a student of late modern (or "postmodern") philosophy to appreciate the elusiveness of self-identity, the fact that we are carriers of a host of identities, many of which derive from identifications by others. More recently, I have learned of the Buddhist notion of "dependent co-arising" (*pratitya samutpada*), an idea signifying that all things come into being simultaneously and interact constantly, in such a manner that it is extremely difficult to separate or lift up one strand as distinguished from all others.

Hence, my hesitations regarding autobiography run deep. Putting them aside required the intervention of well-meaning colleagues and friends. Once I talked with Robert Bernasconi, a philosopher with a fine track record in working on Continental thought (and who, like me, understands well the elusiveness of identity). Prodded by him I told him about my repeated meetings with well-known Western thinkers, including Gadamer, Habermas, Bobbio, Derrida, Foucault, Ricoeur, and others. When, among these thinkers, I also mentioned the name of Carl Schmitt (who recently has gained renewed prominence), he was startled and observed that it was really imperative for me to write down these recollections in a biographical account. I regarded this as a friendly gesture on his part and let the matter rest. More recently, at a conference in New Haven, I met Steven Lukes with whom I had maintained friendly relations since our days in Oxford. In the course of our conversation, he told me also, quite spontaneously, that I should write an autobiography.

Not long afterward, I accidentally came across an autobiographical account that greatly impressed me and further diminished my hesitations. The account was written by the great German-American theologian and philosopher of religion Paul Tillich, who gave it the title *On the Boundary*—quite appropriately. Tillich emigrated to America at the beginning of the Nazi regime, which he detested for both theological and political reasons. His account was written soon after his emigration and strongly bore the imprint of a "hyphenated" life. Although my own departure from Germany occurred twenty years later, I could strongly empathize with his story. As I discovered subsequently, in the course of further readings, Tillich was a boundary-person in many respects, straddling the divide between Barthian orthodoxy and liberal Protestantism, between traditional religious "transcendentalism" and late-modern existentialism and life philosophy. Some of his other writings—when I explored them—strongly resonated with me, texts like *The Courage to Be*, *The New Being*, and *Ultimate Concern*. I trust he will posthumously forgive me for appropriating the title of his biographical account for my own purposes.

Because of these experiences, I began to take more seriously the idea of writing my own account. Initially I thought of writing only a few pages or a short essay; but as the writing progressed, the narrative expanded and became more detailed. Still, it was clear to me that writing such a story is an act of self-interpretation that requires selection: some aspects or episodes had to be foregrounded at the expense of a host of others. I tried to proceed judiciously in this regard but am not sure that I always got it right. Some people whose names are omitted have perhaps played a stronger role than I can now assess; perhaps my assessment will change in other contexts.

After all, interpretation is always finite and contextual; and as in genuine conversation, there is no final voice in storytelling. I have always been fond of the way in which Michel Foucault started his "Discourse on Language" in 1970 at the Collège de France: "I would really like to have slipped imperceptibly into this lecture . . . I would have preferred to be enveloped in words, borne way beyond all possible beginnings. At the moment of speaking, I would like to have perceived a nameless voice, long preceding me, leaving me merely to enmesh myself in it, taking up its cadence, and to lodge myself, when no one was looking, in its interstices as if it had paused an instant, in suspense, to beckon to me."

F. D. Notre Dame
May 2016

Acknowledgments

The reflections are made possible in part by support from the Institute for Scholarship in the Liberal Arts, College of Arts and Letters, University of Notre Dame.

On the Boundary

A Life Remembered

WHOSE LIFE?

How does one, in the twilight years, write down the story of one's life? Whose life is one beginning to tell, and whose story is it? Indeed, it is in a sense one's own life—but the "own-ness" is fragile and perhaps only metaphorical. Does one ever own one's life and can one really tell its story straightforwardly—like a narrator who grasps the central plot? From the beginning, it seems, one's life is entangled in a vast network of other stories, a tangle of other lives, memories of the departed, and tales or legends at the edge of anyone's awareness. So, how does one extricate that thread, or perhaps that bundle of threads, one calls one's life? In telling the story, one realizes quickly that it is part of a bundle of stories—more so: that one is oneself a story told by a narrator who is reticent and reserved and thus does not allow us to become fully familiar with ourselves.

There is another complication involved in telling the story of one's life. As I am writing these lines, I am above eighty years of age. By all accounts, I have lived a long life (and still continue living, for the time being). I am supposed to tell the story from the beginning, from my childhood forward. But actually I am telling it from the vantage of old age backward. Hence, backward and forward moves mingle; past, present and future intersect in a strange symbiosis or playfulness. In his *Remembrance of Things Past*, the French novelist Marcel Proust writes, "The earliest appearances in our lives of a person who is destined to take our fancy later on assume retrospectively in our eyes a certain value as an indication, a warning, a presage."[1] In this passage, Proust alerts us to the non-linear character of lived experience, to

1

the mutual embroilment of temporalities in any present. Somehow, this has always been my experience. My earliest experiences, I recall, were always saturated or inhabited by anticipations or premonitions, by an inkling "presaging" something in the future. That inkling was always quite inchoate or inarticulate, nothing more than a cue—perhaps a certain street corner or a light cast on a roof or a meadow. Without being in any way a maxim or a principle, the cue seemed to exhort me simply to remain on the "way," not to lose my path, to remain faithful to something. Now, in my old age, I have to ask myself: have I been faithful, did I remain on the way, or have I gotten lost? And what was or is that way? Sacred scripture contains a line that says, "Guard your heart with all your strength; for from there springs life."[2] Is that the way?

So, almost inevitably, I approach the story of my life with ambivalence, in a questioning mood: Who is that person about whom I am writing and with whom I somehow, awkwardly, identify? And who are all the others I have encountered throughout the many years? How can I be sure? The philosopher Gabriel Marcel writes that life is not a problem to be solved, but rather a mystery to be lived or be plumbed, with no definite end in sight. We are, he says, somehow "suspended" over that mystery.[3] Surely, there are problems in life we can try to solve to the best of our ability; but our life or our being does not seem to be one of them. So we have to approach our life cautiously, gingerly, always ready for unexpected surprises. This is also the way in which we need to approach the divine; Marcel certainly would have thought so. All those (philosophers or theologians) who claim to know or fully comprehend the divine are surely mistaken, in my view; their doctrines contradict what they affirm. Here, too, we have to proceed cautiously, questioningly, always ready for unexpected surprises. As Nicolaus Cusanus realized: we can only know unknowingly, comprehend incomprehensibly—by simply "searching for the face."[4]

Writing from the vantage of old age has advantages and disadvantages: it has the advantage of affording a longer view, but the disadvantage of forgetfulness and inattention to some details (which may or may not be important). At this stage of my life, I cannot help but ponder some texts written about old age. In his *De Senectude* (On Old Age), Cicero writes, "Nature has given us this dwelling place in which to stop for shelter, not to live in forever. Magnificent will be the day when I shall depart for that divine meeting place and assembly of souls."[5] Although admiring its grand style, I find the text somewhat stilted and too saturated with Stoic aloofness from worldly vicissitudes; moreover, Cicero at the time was only sixty-two. Hence I prefer to turn to another, more recent text written by the Italian philosopher Norberto Bobbio (an important mentor of my younger years). When he was already in his eighties—an age he had reached to his own amazement (as he says)—Bobbio wrote a series of reflections translated as *Old Age and Other Essays*, which are more down-to-earth and free of rhetoric or empty subterfuge. As a responsible thinker, he first of all pondered the social implications of aging today, stating that "old age has become a great social problem that remains unsolved and difficult to solve, not only because of the increased number of old people, but also because of the increased number of years that we live as old people." On a more personal level, he added these sobering and weary comments:

> I would say that mine is a melancholic old age. . . . It [melancholy] corresponds to the view of life as a road, along which the destination constantly shifts further down, and as soon as you reach it, you realize that it is not the final destination you first thought. . . . Melancholy, however, is tempered by the constancy of affections that time has not devoured.[6]

As is commonly agreed, advancing years steadily give added weight to memory or remembrance. Bobbio knew it well. "The world of old people, all old people," he writes, "is to a greater or lesser extent the world of memory. People say that ultimately you are what you have done, thought and loved; I would also say that you are what you can remember."[7] Like life itself, memories are ambivalent. When he was in his seventies (and thus still a bit youngish), the Chinese sage Confucius reflected on the course of his life, noting how it had unfolded or matured over the decades, and concluded with these words: "And at seventy I could give my heart-mind free rein without overstepping the mark."[8] Thus, at this point his natural desires or impulses were in harmony with what is "desirable" or what is needed to maintain the "way." This is a picture of life as something steadily accumulating and reaching final culmination. Sometimes I now feel this way about my own journey. But at other times I waver, even as an octogenarian. There are moments when younger impulses or longings still stir in the depths of my heart, catching me by surprise. Maybe this is not so astonishing and was perhaps familiar to Confucius himself. What is at issue are not so much the promptings, as how one comes to terms with them. When he was in his mid-seventies, the poet Goethe fell (once again) passionately in love—a passion which led to nothing, or rather to the hauntingly moving "Elegy of Marienbad."[9]

But at this point, as I begin my own remembrances, I want to start on a somewhat more upbeat note. I gain support or sustenance from some spiritual teachings, but also from some philosophical or intellectual mentors. I am fond of a saying attributed to the philosopher Edmund Husserl, the founder of modern phenomenology. When he was of advanced age and already quite famous, Husserl is reported to have said, "Now, at last, I feel like a true beginner." Who knows whether the advancing years, and what lies further beyond them, do not presage a new beginning? I am also encouraged by one of Husserl's students or followers, Paul Ricouer, who had a distinct impact on my life. Not long ago, when I was in Paris, I discovered in a bookstore a slender, posthumously edited book by him (he died in 2005, at the age of ninety-two). Its title: *Vivant jusqu'à la Mort* (now translated as *Living Up to Death*). The book is a passionate defense of life—and also a critique of a certain theological glorification of death (as atonement), disregarding its life-giving or life-sustaining potency. As he comments at one point: Death is not the end or denial of life but "the transfer onto the other (or others) of the love of life (*l'amour de la vie*)."[10] This is something, I believe, one needs to learn.

Yet perhaps the final word in this matter needs to go not to philosophers but to poets. Rainer Maria Rilke has been a source of deep inspiration in my youth and of sustenance throughout my life. In a letter of 1915, Rilke stated of one of his early works, "What is expressed in the *Notebook of Malte Laurids Brigge* is simply this: How is it possible to live when the fundamentals of this life are so completely incomprehensible? When we are always inadequate in love, wavering in our determination . . . how is it possible to exist?" Relying on the same *Notebook*, Marcel offers this interpretation: "To give life weight is to weigh things according to the carat measure of the heart, not of suspicion or chance. There must be no denial; quite the reverse: there must be an infinite adherence to *that which is*" (*Zustimmung zum Dasein, Du-Sein, Anders-Sein*).[11]

CHILDHOOD: AUGSBURG

As I am told, I was born on October 18, 1928, in the city of Ulm on the Danube. My birth in that particular city was in a way fortuitous because my parents actually lived in Augsburg. It so happened that my mother at that time was visiting her parents in Ulm, and this is when I arrived. As it seems, however, I was not very eager to arrive because I had to be delivered by way of an operation. Was there perhaps some kind of premonition about this world and what it holds in store? I grew up in Augsburg, a city located between Ulm and Munich. I have always felt lucky about growing up in that place because it offers such a long historical view. The founding of the city goes back to the Roman Emperor Augustus, and archaeological excavations have brought to light a wealth of Roman artifacts (now on display in many parts of town). During the later phase of the Roman period the area was Christianized, and that faith left its deep imprint on the character and physiognomy of the city. For someone interested in medieval history (as I was), it is possible to study and savor the entire sequence of architectural styles by just wandering from church to church: from early Basilica style to Romanesque to Gothic to Baroque. Sometimes the styles are blended, the result of later additions or accretions to earlier buildings.

The period, however, that marked most decisively the character of Augsburg was the age of Renaissance and Reformation. During the Renaissance, learned classical scholars and literary figures (like Konrad Peutinger and von Stadion) thrived in the city. Great architects erected magnificent, well-proportioned structures reminiscent of the Italian style of the period—most famously the city hall (*Rathaus*) designed by Elias Holl. One also needs to recall that the city then was the commercial hub of the so-called Holy Roman Empire, with wealthy merchants like the Fuggers serving as the bankers of emperors and kings. Turmoil and strife entered the city with the Reformation. Augsburg was the site of the famous meeting between Martin Luther

Catholic St. Ulrich and Protestant St. Ulrich in Augsburg.

and the papal emissary Cajetan (when Luther had to flee through a narrow gate which can still be seen). During the strife, the city was ruled alternately by Protestants and Catholics—until the Peace of Augsburg (1555) finally put an end to, or at least softened, confessional rivalries. Subsequently, the city was governed equally by representatives of the two confessions (the so-called *Parität*). I should also mention that, during many centuries, Augsburg was a "free imperial city" not attached to any kingdom or principality, a status that allowed the cultivation of a sense of civic autonomy and self-rule. When the Napoleonic Wars brought an end to the Holy Roman Empire, they also did away with this independent status. Augsburg in due course was incorporated into the kingdom of Bavaria and hence "provincialized." Then followed a period of industrialization and urban expansion, a fact evident in the sprawling suburbs surrounding the inner city today.[12]

I mention this story of the city not out of historical curiosity, but for personal reasons: beyond being a geographical location, the city and its story inhabit my inner space. Like a geological formation, that space is layered in different strata that are distinguishable one from the other but also interact in curious ways. There is in me a love of antiquity that was nurtured in secondary school through the study of Latin and Greek. There are medieval layers, not yet touched by later Romanticism, which come to the fore especially in times of crisis or dejection when reason is not fully able to cope. What protects me from a nostalgic medievalism, however, is my attachment to great Renaissance figures: the sobriety and classical equilibrium of such thinkers as Erasmus, Thomas More, Reuchlin, and others. In turn, what the Reformation unleashed for me were the inner stirrings and aspirations of the individual soul—freed from the constraints of outdated conventions and cumbersome rituals.

Yet here too a certain balance needs to be maintained so that the dimensions of inner and outer, tradition and innovation do not completely drift apart. At least to an extent, such a balance was the goal (or hope) of the Peace of Augsburg, an event celebrated annually in recent centuries. To me, this peace has always symbolized the spirit of interfaith toleration and respect far removed from narrow fundamentalism and exclusivism. In a town enjoying the status of a free imperial city, interfaith tolerance gave a powerful boost to public civility and civic broad-mindedness. Probably it is this legacy that has nurtured in me a fondness for a certain "civic republicanism"—not of the Machiavellian, but the Erasmian kind. Governed equally by different denominations, the city sponsored neither a rigid separation of church and state nor the establishment of one creed; rather, public space was both different from and yet favorable to faith. (Much later I learned that this seems to have been Gandhi's version of a secular regime.)

The concrete historical context of my childhood was grim and dismal. Soon after my birth, the Great Depression struck Europe and the Western world, leaving economies in shambles and millions of people impoverished and unemployed. These events imposed great hardship on my parents, especially due to the near collapse of the real-estate market. Then came the rise of a sinister populist movement that exploited the misery of peoples for its own goal of national glory and racial domination. And finally World War II broke out, triggered by the power lust and racial hatreds of the fascist movement, a war leaving much of Germany as well as many other countries in ruins. Given these circumstances, one would assume that my childhood—or any childhood—during these years was bound to be dark and miserable. Strangely, this was not my immediate experience; my own childhood was relatively happy and peaceful. Two protective shields guarded me. One was the calm and harmonious quality of Augsburg whose varied dimensions offered ample room for the growth of mind and imagination. The other, still more important factor was the shelter of a stable family, of loving parents and siblings. Both of these protective shields were severely tested and even damaged during the war when the older male members of my family were inducted into military service—my oldest brother never returned from Russia—and when in 1943 Augsburg was firebombed by the Allies, devastating much of the inner city. Even these horrible events, however, did not manage to entirely extinguish the silent glow exuding from my childhood, a glow that would never cease to illuminate my adult years.[13]

In a way, my parents' background is a reflection of the geography of Augsburg, its location between the old kingdoms of Bavaria and Württemberg. My father's side comes mainly from Bavaria, whereas my mother's family hails from Württemberg. Bavaria (at least Upper Bavaria) has traditionally been Catholic, whereas Württemberg has been denominationally mixed with a strong Lutheran presence. As it seems, my father's ancestors inhabited the lake country south of Munich and Augsburg; his forebears were mainly fishermen, merchants, and clergymen (one even served as abbot in a monastery of the area). My father himself was a realtor, a member of the lower middle class; although coming from a Catholic background, he professed to be religiously "unmusical," by which he meant agnostic. His pragmatic outlook prompted him to shy away from spiritual issues, which (to him) were out of touch with real-life experience. Yet he never argued against religious beliefs or discouraged religious leanings in his wife or children.

He did not in any way object when my older brother decided to enter the seminary to study for the priesthood. Maybe he realized that it would not take hold—an expectation borne out when, after only two years, my brother left the seminary and went to Munich to study history and literature. On my mother's side, parents and grandparents were either Catholic or Protestant; often there were "mixed" marriages. This legacy of mixture is what struck me in my mother's case—who was religious or rather spiritual in her own way without strict adherence to church rituals. Probably it was her very personal spirituality that made her particularly comfortable with Protestant (pietistic) friends and pastors who often visited our home—though without any animus against people of other denominations. Although I received first communion rather than confirmation, she encouraged us to attend both Catholic and Protestant services to broaden our religious horizons.

In their temperament our parents were quite different. Whereas father was sober, business-like, and steady, our mother was more spirited or animated, fond of literature, poetry, and storytelling. The two seem to have complemented each other harmoniously; they were faithfully married for more than fifty years, in good and bad times. I never in my life heard them argue with each other or use harsh language. I never witnessed temper tantrums; nor did they argue or quarrel with us—or we with them. The latter had to do with a certain disposition on our part (certainly on my part) to respect our parents fully and to honor their opinions and instructions even if we did not entirely comprehend or perhaps agree with them. In retrospect, it appears that I followed the rules of what the Chinese call "filial piety," which Confucius articulated when he stated, "In relating to parents, a young person may gently remonstrate with them; but if he/she cannot change their opinion, the person should resume an attitude of deference and not offend them."[14] This maxim, I fear, is widely ignored today when families often resemble battlefields. Even when the maxim is known or remembered, it is rarely put into practice. But as Confucius would have said, the point is not to know rules, but to follow the way.

SCHOOL YEARS

My early education was joyful and nurturing. At age six I entered a primary school located near the cathedral (the so-called *Domschule*). Our main teacher was a warm-hearted man who traveled every day on bicycle to school from a nearby village. His surname was Seelentag (Soul Day), a fitting name whom I remember as a kind and "soulful" man—but who could also be stern and use discipline when the occasion called for it. Near the cathedral there was a large park with many tall trees and bushes. In the afternoon, my friends and I would often go to the park, play hide-and-seek, and climb on the trees for cover. There was a plain-clothes detective, however, who would inspect the park, take down our names, and report them to our school. Hence, at least twice a week, our teacher would lecture us, in the presence of the detective, about the importance of keeping public places in good order and undefiled so that citizens could enjoy them in peace. The lectures made some sense but not enough to deter us. Moreover, even when he was sternly reprimanding us, I thought I detected a subdued smile in our teacher, suggesting that perhaps there needed to be room for both order and youthful pranks.

After I attended four years of elementary school my parents decided to send me to a classical secondary school (*humanistisches Gymnasium*). I am not sure what prompted their decision; maybe just a hunch. There were at the time two such classical schools in Augsburg; one was Protestant or Lutheran (St. Anna) and the other Catholic or Benedictine (St. Stephan). For some reason, the Catholic school had gotten into trouble with the regime at the beginning of the war (when I was ten) and was closed for several years. Hence, I went to St. Anna, a place of some historical significance because of the visit of Martin Luther and also the tomb of the Fuggers in the crypt of the church. We started the study of Latin in the first grade and Greek in the third grade; modern languages would follow later. I was again fortunate in having good and dedicated teachers—whom, I regret to say, we repaid too often with all kinds of mischief. Our teacher in Latin and history was a Dr. Schuhmacher (Shoemaker); but we called him "*Schupo*" (policeman)—which was a very unfair description in light of his gentle and forgiving nature. When we were particularly unruly in class, he would call us *Landsknechte* (medieval mercenaries)—the harshest expression in his vocabulary but a very harmless and innocuous term in our ears. The director of the school was a distinguished man by the name of Dr. Heim. In him I encountered for the first time the kind of Lutheran pietism that later I would explore with considerable interest. He would often visit our home and have long discussions with my mother.

My entry into St. Anna coincided with the beginning of World War II. I vividly recall this moment. In late summer of 1939 I happened to be in an open-air swimming facility attached to a large playground. Suddenly, in the midst of a game of table tennis, a voice boomed over the public loudspeaker: "Germany has declared war; the invasion of Poland has begun." I recall the deep shock occasioned by these words. I had no notion of war, but the announcement was full of dark, ominous forebodings. Then followed the series of lightning invasions of which the regime would boast—as well as a tightening of internal regimentation in the name of national security. In our class in St. Anna, there was a Jewish boy, Fritz Reisinger, who was a good classmate and a friend to many of us. Suddenly one day we were informed that he and his family were moving elsewhere and he would no longer be with us. We interpreted this as a simple relocation, thinking that maybe his father had been transferred. Should we have probed more fully? Should we have asked directly where they were heading? The idea that they would be sent to a concentration camp simply did not occur to me. Who would even contemplate such horrible things? The regime certainly did not publicize its atrocities to ordinary citizens. The entire horror of the Holocaust did not truly become apparent to me until after the war. I was aghast, unable to fathom it. I am still unable to fathom it. How could this happen among presumably civilized people?

The war had a deep and disrupting impact on our family, as it did everywhere. My father, then in his forties, was enlisted in the military as a quartermaster and spent some time in France. My eldest brother Albert (born 1919) served in the infantry and was sent to Russia. In 1943, during one of the devastating battles in central Russia, he was reported missing in action; we never heard from him again. My other brother Horst, two years older than me, was required while still in high school to serve as "helper" in an anti-aircraft battery located at the outskirts of Augsburg. From his location he could observe in 1943 the entire drama of the fire-bombing of Augsburg, which left much of the inner city in ruins. I myself spent the war alone with my mother at home. Several pupils at St. Anna who lived nearby were required to spend some nights every week in school in order to assist in case of fire. I recall that many times, when things were quiet, we would play hide-and-seek in the dark corridors and classrooms. I was at school during the night of the massive five-bombing. Initially we stayed in the cellar; when we emerged, the entire sky was red and the air filled with smoke. After we helped to combat some fires under the roof, we were allowed to go home. The street on which we lived was a disaster. The houses on both sides of the street were empty shells, with fires still raging inside and the outer walls collapsing into the street. I had to climb carefully over the debris to reach my house—which miraculously was still standing. Apart from gratitude for this saving grace, that night has instilled in me a profound revulsion against war, a revulsion deepened by all the other horrors of the war about which I learned later. As Erasmus has said, citing Pindar: "War is appealing only to those who do not know it (*dulce bellum inexpertis*)."[15]

In retrospect, I cannot exaggerate the importance of these war years for my subsequent intellectual and political development. I feel that, in large measure, I can trace my persistent opposition to war and violence—especially aggressive warfare—to this youthful experience. The war years forced me to become sober and to put aside a certain childish utopianism; but they did not dent my hope for the future and my trust in the better side of humanity. I know that a similar sober hope was shared by many people at the time. The immediate postwar years were for many—especially people of my generation—a time of intense soul-searching, stock-taking, existential anxiety, and perhaps inner awakening. The churches in town, which during the Nazi years had been mostly empty, were suddenly filled to capacity or overflowing. Charismatic preachers would address large crowds, calling them back from the abyss of national degradation unto the path of religious faith and righteousness. On certain holidays, huge processions were held through the streets of Augsburg, attended by both Catholics and Protestants (and perhaps some agnostics). It was a time of great intellectual and social ferment, also a time when ideas coming from abroad—and previously excluded—were suddenly flooding the country and filling our minds. I recall especially the immense popularity of French existentialism and of French cinema and plays, especially the plays and movies of Jean-Paul Sartre and the novels of Albert Camus.[16] At the same time, recent British and American literary works exerted great influence. I remember especially being captivated by Thornton Wilder's *Our Town* and *The Ides of March*.

The end of the war occasioned a shift in my education. Apparently because of some suspected complicity, St. Anna was closed for a time while the Benedictine school of St. Stephan reopened. Together with a number of classmates I transferred in 1945 to the latter school. I never regretted that shift because the educational climate at St. Stephan was superb. The school was guided then by a number of older, experienced Benedictine teachers

Pater Gregor Lang, rector of St. Stephan in Augsburg (1924-1939, 1945-1962); photo St. Stephan Archives.

whose competence and pedagogical skills were outstanding. My teacher in Greek and in literature was a man whom I cannot praise highly enough: Pater Gregor Lang. He was a kind and gentle person but also a gifted teacher who challenged us to perform at the top of our ability. I am still sitting in his classroom, the air filled with sublime verses from Homer, Hesiod, and Sophocles. What a total change from the barbaric desolation of the Nazi regime.

Near the school and monastery there was (and still is) a beautiful garden surrounded by high walls. Pater Gregor would often invite me there for some walks and some closer readings of Sophocles and Plato. There is one other thing I need to mention about him. Although a Catholic priest, Pater Gregor was deeply fond of Goethe and delighted us with readings from Goethe's poetry and prose writings. When I asked him about the seeming incongruity, he smiled and said that faith and good literature are twins. Much later I would learn about Erasmus's maxim of *fides et eruditio*. There was indeed a gentle Erasmian piety among the Benedictine monks at the time. We also had fine teachers in Latin, English, mathematics, and music—to mention only the topics I liked best. (Today, like most of these schools, St. Stephan is largely secularized because of a shortage of novices.)

A number of other people entered or surrounded my life during the years at St. Stephan. One was a gifted artist priest who served as monsignor to the bishop of Augsburg. His name was Dr. Josef Kunstmann. Because of his somewhat eccentric flamboyance he had a strong impact on many young men in the city. His religious outlook was not at all Benedictine or Erasmian but rather existentialist and Augustinian—with an emphasis on the lostness, anxiety, and torn-ness of human life. In the midst of the ruins of postwar Germany, this outlook had an aura of authenticity that captured us—up to a point. Once I confronted Pater Gregor with this stark difference in attitudes. He calmly told me that there is indeed suffering, which we must not forget, but that despite torment there is also the longing for joy and happiness.[17]

Another person, still more important to me in the long run, was a young man by the name of Robert Bernhardt who joined us at St. Stephan and subsequently became my lifelong companion and friend. His family was not well-to-do and his father had passed away some time ago; so he had to take on odd jobs to support his mother and himself (at one point he worked for American troops stationed in the city). Apart from the wartime and postwar malaise, Robert had a sobering effect on me. He was slightly older than me (the age of my middle brother) and hence a bit more mature. When looking at me, he seemed to look not just at the boy I was, but at something hidden (hidden also to me): perhaps some latent potential or possibility. Thus, being with him was not just enjoyable but also beckoning or enticing—toward untapped horizons. How can one ever sufficiently praise a friendship like this?

These postwar years also taught me about changing fortunes and how quickly political power or might—seemingly invincible at one point—can vanish overnight. In the aftermath of the bombing of Augsburg I had been required, together with other boys, to appear periodically at some emergency center to assist in various tasks. One time, I was a bit late because of some pressing things at home. At the center I was received by a party official (actually a ranking leader of the youth organization) who proceeded to reprimand me sternly and in the end to slap my face repeatedly in anger. Needless to say, I was not pleased. Toward the end of my school years I took on a few jobs to help my family. One such job was with the main local newspaper. I served in an office open to the public where people would come to place ads in the paper. One day the same ranking official, now a civilian, appeared in the office in order to place an ad. I gave him a paper to fill out, which he did. It turned out he was looking for a job, any job whatever. I am not sure whether he recognized me. Looking at him and still remembering his earlier impressive uniform, I found that he looked ragged, disheveled, and dispirited. Never having had a heart for vengeance, I took the ad and handed it to my supervisors at the paper.

During these years I also became quite proficient at the piano, which I had been studying since I was ten or eleven. I had a very good teacher, a Mr. Adolf Menzel, who also played the harp in the local opera house, and by my late teens I was giving recitals in small circles. There was (and still is) a large synagogue in Augsburg that somehow had not been damaged during the war. During the postwar years, a small Jewish community emerged again at that location, including a fine and cultured man named Adam Mishkin. He was an accomplished violinist who had learned of my piano playing and proceeded to invite me to his home next to the synagogue. He asked me whether I was willing to accompany him, and I was delighted by this opportunity.

From then on, for more than half a year, we would meet weekly and practice together. We played mainly the violin concerto by Max Bruch and also a Tchaikovsky concerto. (Actually, we played the Bruch concerto so often that even today I feel a bit saturated.) Sometimes we would give recitals. One time, on a special Jewish holiday, we played our music to a larger Jewish gathering. I remember that one member of the audience asked Mishkin how he could play with a young German after all that had happened. He simply shrugged and said, "Well, he was too young to know and, moreover, he is a good pianist." Mishkin also took me occasionally to a Sabbath service in the synagogue.[18] I was struck by the different manner of reading scriptures from what I had observed in Christian churches. Much later, during my travels in the Middle East and Asia, I would attend the services or rites of different religious communities, thereby extending my horizons and also learning how different faiths complement each other.

LEGAL STUDIES: MUNICH AND BRUSSELS

I graduated from secondary school in 1948. (Because of the turbulence at the end of the war, school schedules had been somewhat disrupted or delayed.) My piano teacher thought that I should continue practicing and eventually become a concert pianist. Although slightly attracted to this idea, I felt that this course of action would seriously hamper and perhaps stymie my intellectual ambitions or concerns. Others suggested that I should attend the university—but to study what? Uncertain and deeply troubled by my uncertainty, I chose to postpone the decision and to do a few other things in the meantime. One was to work in the newspaper office.

I also served as apprentice to a master carpenter who lived in a castle near Augsburg, a friend of my father's. I worked very hard—and had to do so because of a lack of native talent. At the end of about four months I was able to fabricate by myself a small night stand of which I was quite proud—but which my brother (who was much more talented in this respect) found laughable.[19] So I moved on. My next station was at a printing shop owned by an aunt or great-aunt in Riedlingen in Württemberg. At that time printing, in its initial phase, was still done entirely by hand, which means that a text had to be set letter by letter (one took the letters out of a large tray and put them one by one into a hand-held composing stick). Since I was very fond of Rilke—I was particularly moved by his *Duino Elegies* and his *Sonnets to Orpheus*—I proceeded to assemble the *Sonnets* letter by letter and to have the text run off on the printing machine (I still have some copies).[20]

After several such excursions into trade, the decision could not be postponed much longer. Following the lead of some classmates in secondary school, I embarked on the study of law or jurisprudence at the University of Munich. Actually, I followed not only their lead but also a certain inchoate interest on my part. Without fully realizing it, I have always been interested in public or political matters—not in raw power politics but in the ethical or normative dimension, that is, the point where politics and philosophical reflection meet. At the time, this kind of concern was addressed in German universities in the faculty of law or jurisprudence. German law faculties were very different from American law schools, which are much more narrowly technical and professionalized. Legal studies in Germany were part of the Roman civil law tradition (as opposed to the British-American common law tradition) and they gave relatively broad room to philosophical, historical, and humanistic dimensions of law. Among the courses I had to take, I favored the topics of natural law, philosophy of law, historical jurisprudence, and also constitutional law—while the mandatory lessons in contract law, tort, and criminal law left me frustrated and mentally fatigued. As is evident, the latter topics are the "bread-and-butter" courses needed by future practicing lawyers—which should have given me a cue early on.[21]

Apart from attending law courses or classes by the resident legal faculty, I made it a point to sample courses or lectures offered in other faculties of the university. Particularly impressive to me were courses offered in Munich by the great philosopher-theologian Romano Guardini. In his sober and balanced presentation of the relation between faith and reason I detected again the gentle Erasmian spirit that had nurtured me in secondary school. Also, his reflections on the relation between faith and politics or the public domain provided food for thought for a young generation trying to find a new beginning after so many disasters. Memorable for me were also the classes given by the great historian Franz Schnabel on such topics as the Reformation, the religious wars, and the age of Enlightenment. Here lines of historical development were clearly delineated that had been disrupted or mangled by the sudden outbreak of barbarism. Because Munich at the time was also a hub of intellectual and artistic life (given that Berlin was reduced to an enclave or island), many foreign luminaries came there and presented talks in the overflowing *Aula* (auditorium) of the university. Still particularly vivid in my recollection are repeated appearances of the great Spanish philosopher Ortega y Gasset. In his public lectures, a whole new world of ideas and perspectives flooded into our hearts and minds—ideas having to do with existentialism, phenomenology, and life philosophy as well as with liberalism, communism, and humanism.

During my Munich years I also had an encounter with the prominent legal and constitutional thinker Carl Schmitt, who was reemerging at the time into the public limelight. Schmitt had been an important legal and political theorist during the Weimar Republic but subsequently had become embroiled with the Nazi regime (the precise extent of this embroilment was not clear to me then, nor is it entirely clear to me now). After the war, like many other intellectuals, he went through a period of soul-searching and (perhaps) inner spiritual renewal. Some evidence of this inner drama emerged in such postwar books as *Ex Captivitate Salus, Donoso Cortés*, and *Der Nomos der Erde*, all published in 1950. It was this string of publications that attracted my attention and aroused my desire to meet with him. I wrote to him and he promptly invited me to visit him at his home in the small town of Plettenberg in Westphalia. He received me graciously and we had lunch together with his daughter. Following lunch he took me for a long walk in the beautiful countryside (it was summer). We talked about many things but especially the work of Thomas Hobbes. As he told me, what he liked most in Hobbes was his political candor or toughness: his insistence on the need for "sovereign" power as the final arbiter. He also valued Hobbes's maxim that it is authority or power, not truth or ethics, which determines the content of law (*auctoritas not veritas facit legem*). When I cautiously reminded him of Hobbes's concessions to natural law (*pax est quaerenda*), he brushed them aside as irrelevant to the core of the argument.[22] Here I discovered a rift between us on which much later I would try to elaborate.

After four years of studies, law students had to pass a final state examination in all legal fields. That examination was approached by students with dread because of its comprehensiveness and reputed toughness. It was customary for students to engage special tutors for several months; I followed that custom. The exam came—and to my great amazement and relief I passed. Now a new quandary or decision loomed ahead of me: Should I continue with the pursuit of a legal career—which, at that time, meant spending four more years as an intern in courts and administrative offices? Not cherishing this prospect but also not knowing what to do, I postponed the matter by deciding to write a doctoral dissertation. There was at the time a distinguished professor in the Munich law faculty by the name of Hans Nawiasky. He taught mainly constitutional law and aspects of international law and was reputed to be the father of the postwar Bararian constitution. I had a good relationship with him, although contact was difficult; he lived in Switzerland and commuted to his classes. Regarding the choice of topic, I took my bearings from recent developments in Europe: the emergence of the first fledgling common European institutions (such as the Coal and Steel Community and the Assembly in Strasbourg). In discussions with Nawiasky, we agreed that I would write on a theme tentatively called "The Idea of the 'Supra-National' in Modern International Law." As one should note, modern international law is basically an interstate law, that is, a normative order established contractually between nation-states and not in principle challenging the sovereignty of these states. (This was even true of the League of Nations and continues to be the case in the United Nations.) Thus, the emergence of supra-national institutions seemed to me to inaugurate a new dispensation, pointing perhaps in the direction of a shared "law of peoples" (*ius gentium*).[23]

In trying to write a dissertation, the first step is always extensive research and consultation with experts in the field. I was lucky to receive a year-long stipend from my university to conduct the required research. I chose to do the latter in Brussels, Belgium, because of the presence there of a well-known teacher of international law by the name of Henri Rolin (an acquaintance of Nawiasky). Professor Rolin received me very warmly and agreed to assist me in some of my work. He taught at the so-called Free University (*Université Libre*) in Brussels, and I attended some of his classes there. I should add that Rolin was simultaneously a member of the Belgian Senate and divided his time between his classes and his senatorial obligations. I have always greatly admired this ability to combine academic pursuits with public service— something that has become all too rare today (and which I myself have not been able to emulate). The Free University in Brussels is a Francophone institution, and thus I was able to improve my French proficiency along the way. As the name indicates, the university is also an emphatically progressive and secular institution—an aspect which sets it off against the Flemish-speaking Catholic university there. I have never been greatly troubled by secularism as such and actually find that a certain non-aggressive version of it can also be beneficial to religious people (by teaching them about tolerance and civic respect). Thanks to my interaction with Rolin and some good library facilities, I was able to make good progress on my dissertation and, on my return from Brussels, was already well into the writing stage.[24]

What remained to be done was the final composing and revising of the thesis, followed by a doctoral exam. The practice in Munich was a *viva* (oral) defense in front of Nawiasky and the doctoral committee. The defense went well—although it was punctuated by some tense moments. As should be recalled, my thesis was basically a plea for supra-nationality, that is, for a legal or normative regime transgressing the narrow bounds of state sovereignty. As I had expected (or had been forewarned), there were some eyebrows raised by traditional lawyers and also by international "realists" skeptical of any tampering with sovereign prerogatives. In retrospect I can say that these kinds of skeptical queries or objections have accompanied me throughout my life and I have developed reasonably plausible or cogent responses to them. At the time of my defense, it was mainly Nawiasky's academic prestige and authority that settled the issue in my favor. Thus, after some of the usual formalities had been taken care of, I finally received the title of *Doctor juris* or Doctor of Law (actually of "both laws," civil and canon, "*utriusque legis*"). This happened in summer of 1955. With this, one course of action was completed. But what was completely unresolved was the question: What to do next?

TURIN: EUROPEAN INSTITUTE

The dissertation stipend for my stay in Brussels was only for one year (1953–54), so I needed to look around for follow-up opportunities. This was the time of the beginning of European unification—a process that opened up new opportunities for young people to work in the emerging European institutions or agencies. To prepare young people for this kind of work, programs called something like "Institutes of European Studies" sprang up in several parts of the Continent. I applied to one in Turin, Italy, and, to my joy, was accepted into their program. Thus, while still putting the final touches to my thesis, I went to Turin during 1954–55. I have always been deeply fond of Italy and, already during my student days in Munich, managed to escape ever so often to the "sunny South." This was one of my reasons for choosing the Italian institute. Located in hilly Piedmont and traversed by the river Po, Turin is a lovely city with wide streets lined by trees and arcades—although a bit on the austere or formal side. The city is the home of the former royal family of Savoy and still exudes some of the traditional aura. One of its churches houses the famous "shroud"—which I often looked at without quite knowing what to make of it.

Turin became for me a very important place: Although I had chosen it for a somewhat whimsical reason (my affection for Italy), it was there that the future course of my life was in a way charted. Although located in Piedmont, the instruction given at the Institute and the work done there was in French. The teachers and also the students (all postgraduates) came from different parts of Europe, from North to South. Since the basic point of the Institute was to prepare students for public service in European institutions, instruction ranged over many disciplines, from politics, law, and economics to history and literature. I greatly appreciated this interdisciplinary and intercultural education because it gave me a glimpse of the emerging European community (then limited to Western Europe, due to the Cold War). I enjoyed the camaraderie among students and occasionally contributed to the Institute's student-run journal. [25]

The one interest of mine that was not served at the Institute was philosophy, particularly political philosophy. Through acquaintances it came to my attention that there was a teacher at the University of Turin who was widely renowned as a philosopher and especially political philosopher. His name: Norberto Bobbio. Since the university was not far from where I lived, I decided to attend some of Bobbio's lectures—and was enthralled (my Italian being just good enough to understand). A bit later, I went to his office and introduced myself, telling him about my background and my anxious search for a proper path of life. To my great amazement—I am still surprised today—that distinguished professor listened to me attentively and subsequently proceeded to take me under his wings. He became my genuine mentor: by showing me a possible path of life, not by admonition but by example.

As I came to realize—at first only intuitively but then more and more clearly—Bobbio did not just teach philosophy but lived it. Philosophizing or thinking for him was not just a métier or profession but an inner need that permeated his life. At the time, his work concentrated mainly on Hegel, the Left Hegelians, and Marx—every time with a slant toward their relevance for a modern democratic regime. A strong opponent of totalitarianism of any kind, but also not a devotee of laissez-faire liberalism or individualism, his writings charted a course that transgressed ideological Cold War slogans and thus opened a space for innovative political thinking. It was particularly this latter aspect that fascinated me and became a beacon in my own later endeavors. Bobbio's lectures and writings also paid close attention to legal philosophy (something that resonated with my earlier legal studies). I did not share his fondness for the so-called pure theory of law initiated in prior decades by Hans Kelsen; but this divergence was at most a minor footnote in an otherwise deep intellectual convergence.[26] I should add that later Bobbio combined his role as university teacher with service in the Italian Senate (thus paralleling the example of Henri Rolin). At some point, he became a Senator for Life, always acting as a dissident or gadfly in both right-wing and left-wing regimes—a role eminently suitable for a congenitally Socratic thinker.

Although he was not formally connected with the Institute, I learned soon that Bobbio himself was a strong supporter of European unification. At the time, he was deeply involved in what he called "the politics of culture." He was one of the founding members of the European Society of Culture, a society established in 1950 that sought to act as a counterpoise to national politics, or a politics governed by *raison d'Etat*. The organization believed in advancing a transnational ethical force (or rather nonforce) rooted in civil society. Among other founding members were such prominent figures as Hans Urs van Balthazar, Henri Lefebvre, and André Siegfried. Later on, the Society was joined by such intellectuals as the philosopher Jean Wahl, the Dominican Leo van Breda, and the Catalan poet Josep Carner. Basically, the Society opposed the division of Europe signaled by the rise of the Iron Curtain and, more generally, the division of the world into hostile camps

Norberto Bobbio, Italian philosopher at the University of Turin (1909-2004); photo Archivio Norberto Bobbio.

during the Cold War. For one of the meetings of the Society (which I was not able to attend), Bobbio prepared a speech whose text became available to me in excerpts later. Titled "What the European Society of Culture Has Meant for Me," the speech zeroed in on the central issue, stating, "We are faced with the great problem of our times: the division of the world into opposing blocs. The European Society of Culture does not acknowledge this division. Its members have expressed their will not to be subject to one or the other, and favor an attitude that we have defined as 'both over here and over there.'" As Bobbio added, the idea was not to form a "Third Force" governed by the same dictates of power politics as the two blocs but rather to cultivate an ethical disposition designed to curb the potential violence of states. [27]

Without my being aware of it at the time, this idea of a civil-society counterpoise to power politics would much later become one of my own cherished notions. The idea has an Erasmian ring—which is not entirely fortuitous and leads me back to Turin. It so happens that Erasmus received a doctorate in theology from Turin University in 1506; a plaque at the old university building commemorates this fact. In Bobbio's words, "If we had wanted to choose a patron saint [for the city], we could not do better than to choose Erasmus, who had asserted the need for dialogue between opposing sides during the years of religious wars that left Europe in blood." [28] Another famous name associated with Turin is Friedrich Nietzsche. I frequently visited the piazza where Nietzsche is said to have defended a horse from being beaten by its driver and subsequently had a mental breakdown. I cherish this image of a Nietzsche fervently compassionate for mistreated animals. More generally, I am inclined toward philosophers who keep their thinking in touch with their feelings or passions—provided the latter do not run rampant. It is on this point that I am not entirely at ease with Nietzsche. Although admiring his brand of "lived" philosophy (or life philosophy), my attitude toward him has always been ambivalent—maybe because of my fondness for the Erasmian spirit.

TO AMERICA AND BACK

My postgraduate stipend in Turin extended to two years. However, already during my first year at the Institute, the example of Norberto Bobbio had stimulated my desire to explore the possibility of a return to university life. I did not abandon the pursuit of European studies but felt that a temporary return would enable me subsequently to make an informed choice between academia and public service. Out of curiosity—and perhaps in order to keep the two options clearly distinct—I had applied to various American universities for a one-year fellowship; several responded positively. Not being familiar with the country and not having long-range interests, I picked a university that seemed reasonably centrally located to permit exploration of that vast continent. Again, my choice was whimsical—but what happened then was far from whimsical. The place I picked was Southern Illinois University located in the Midwest, in Carbondale. When I arrived there, my interest in studying was somewhat limited, taking a backseat to my planned tourist endeavors. However, officials at the university pointed out to me that, if I added a few summer courses, I could receive a master's degree in one year. I was not entirely sure what I would do with such a degree (especially if later I should decide to go back to Europe). But on reflection the idea made sense: after all, it would give me that close-up academic experience that I desired. At that point I needed to choose a structured field of study in which to pursue the degree. Without fully knowing the ramifications, I choose the field of political theory or philosophy—mainly because it is located midway between politics and pure philosophy, and also because that field had been so compellingly exemplified for me by Bobbio.

As it turned out, this was a good choice, particularly at SIU. One of my teachers of political theory was a dedicated and inspiring younger man by the name of Julius Paul. In his classes I experienced vividly what college education at its best can be—and actually often is in the United States: a friendly, dialogical interaction between teachers and students that triggers a mutual learning experience. That kind of animated interaction, I felt, was very often missing in German universities where the old professorial system tended to erect a gulf between teachers and students. (There are exceptions, of course, and I was fortunate to encounter some of them.) Julius Paul specialized in a number of topics, but especially in the philosophy and sociology of law. In dealing with these themes—and also with the broader tradition of political thought—he adopted a pragmatic approach, loosely inspired by John Dewey. It was in his lectures that I first became acquainted with that important American tradition.

Actually, in favoring a pragmatic approach, Paul was in a way swimming against the tide: As I discovered later, pragmatism by that time had been overtaken in America by logical positivism and analytical philosophy—to his regret (which soon also became my regret). Curiously, during these years, Carbondale became a hub of pragmatic resistance to the dominant currents. It was at SIU—about a decade after my departure—that all of the works of John Dewey were collected and edited by a team of able pragmatic philosophers led by Jo Ann Boydston.[29] What attracted me to pragmatism, especially as presented by Julius Paul, was the endeavor to link together theory and practice, thought and concrete experience, and thus to develop a modern practical philosophy (somewhat in the Aristotelian and Hegelian tradition.)

Carbondale became important and even crucial for me also in another sense. In a way, theoretical studies and lived experience came together on a very personal level: I encountered a young woman there who later became my wife. Her name was Ilse Balzer and she was a student of journalism. Together with her entire extended family, she had emigrated as a young girl from Yugoslavia. Her family came from a German-speaking farming village near Belgrade, a village going back in time to the extensive settlement programs pursued by Empress Maria Theresa of Hapsburg in the Balkans. At the end of the war, the area was a cauldron of strife. Due to persistent attacks by communist partisans, all German-speaking people were forced to flee their homes and villages. Ilse's family first fled to Austria, to a town near Salzburg, in the hope of making a living there. When this proved impossible, they all decided to move to America where they first settled in Oregon and later in and around St. Louis. Later on, I came to know her entire family and was greatly impressed by their diligence and habit of hard work: although arriving in America with little or nothing, they had acquired sizable tracts of land and also new machinery to plow and harvest the fields. It was from St. Louis that Ilse came to Carbondale for her studies; we met and soon a casual acquaintance matured into affection and love. With some hyperbole I liked to think that, in our relationship, we managed to move Western and Eastern Europe closer together. We also tended to complement each other in other ways. Since my childhood, I had always been a "city boy" relatively unfamiliar with the countryside, whereas she had lived in farming communities whose sober lifestyle puts city glitter in proper perspective.

My appointment in Carbondale was only for one year, and I had promised my parents to return home to discuss earnestly my future course of action. So I returned to Europe in late summer of 1956, both for the purpose of this discussion and to complete my second year at the Turin Institute. The issue before me was still the same: to pursue the path of European civil service (for which my legal training and my stay in Turin seemed to prepare me) or else to choose an academic career (whose attractiveness had been demonstrated to me by Bobbio and my experiences in Carbondale). In the end, the second option won out. I have often been asked what prompted me to emigrate to America from Germany—especially at that time when that country was economically booming (a result of the Marshall Plan and the so-called economic miracle). In retrospect, I can only say that a number of factors were at work. One of them was my dismay with the things that happened during the Nazi regime. Another was the uninviting condition of German universities and their old professorial system—a system that was aggravated by the steadily shrinking number of professors and the steadily expanding number of students (this was particularly true in the social sciences and humanities, since all available funds were channeled into natural science and technology). A further factor was a nagging doubt concerning my suitability for a legal or administrative career.

To be truthful, however, all these considerations were outweighed and brushed aside by the inner voice of affection—a voice that became more and more pressing and commanding during the year of separation. In the course of an increasingly frequent exchange of letters, Ilse and I decided that we wanted to get married, preferably in America. To make this possible, I proceeded—while still spending my second year in Turin—to apply for admission and a fellowship at several American universities. This time I chose not on the basis of geography but of acknowledged scholarly reputation (for which I solicited the advice of American friends). The most attractive offer was made to me by a university located in the American South: Duke University in North Carolina, which then boasted a very distinguished faculty in political science and philosophy (it still does today). So this became the next station in my life.

RETURN TO AMERICA

My parents—with whom I had discussed the entire matter—were not eager to see me leave because it involved a separation for long periods. (At that time, one still traveled by ship—which was expensive and took at least a week.) However, after telling them about my career objectives and my eagerness to get married, they consented and wished me well. In late August of 1957, I set out again for the New World, traveling from Genoa through Gibraltar and the Azores to New York. The idea was for us to get married soon after my arrival and before the start of the fall semester. Here I have to tell a little story which to me seems significant. My father had just enough money to pay for my sea voyage; my university stipend was small and a wedding was imminent. My father had written to an acquaintance in New York asking him for help. The acquaintance was a Jewish businessman who earlier had lived in Augsburg and been on good terms with my father. The businessman quickly responded in positive terms—something that amazed me given the horrors of the Nazi regime and what he himself must have gone through as a result. On my arrival in New York I went to his office and he proceeded to give me a loan, without interest, stipulating the precise manner in which he expected to be repaid. During the ensuing year, we carefully followed his instructions and paid back the loan in monthly installments. This was a great help to us but also a good lesson in bookkeeping and financial management.

From New York I traveled by train to St. Louis where the wedding took place, as we had planned. There was to be no honeymoon because the beginning of the fall semester was imminent. So, after the wedding, my wife and I traveled south to Durham in North Carolina where Duke University is located. Without great difficulty we found an apartment in a larger house owned by a pleasant family, not very far from campus. For me, an immediate task was to select classes for the semester and, more generally, a line of emphasis during the years of my graduate work. Given my prior experiences, this emphasis was going to be placed in some way on the theoretical and normative dimension of the study of politics. As it seemed to me then, this focus occupies a midpoint between two opposed perspectives: a purely abstract mode of philosophizing and an untheoretical, fact-gathering type of empiricism.

As I indicated before, American philosophy departments at that time were in the grip of two European imports (both at odds with American pragmatism): logical positivism deriving from the Vienna School, and language analysis and analytical philosophy deriving from England. This predominance implied a nearly complete neglect of the domains of ethics, aesthetics, and politics. On the other hand, the social sciences—including political science—were largely under the sway of a fact-gathering empiricism (called behaviorism or behavioralism) animated by the ambition to remold social studies in the image of natural science. In application to my own path of graduate studies, this situation meant that I needed to find a more congenial, humanistic treatment of the study of politics, combining it with a sampling of courses from adjacent disciplines like philosophy, history, and literature.

Fortunately for me, most of the teachers of political science at Duke University favored this humanistic approach. Among the classes I attended were courses in modern international law offered by a nationally renowned expert (Robert Wilson) who not only was fully knowledgeable about, but deeply committed to a regime of international norms. Under his tutelage, I encountered again that international or supra-national spirit that had guided me in my earlier studies in Munich and Brussels. Another teacher was a well-known expert in comparative politics (Taylor Cole) who approached his field not so much from an empirical or behavioral angle but from a normative perspective, more specifically the perspective of comparative constitutional law. Maybe because of my European background, I served as his research assistance for nearly two years, delving into important decisions handed down by the German and Austrian high courts.

More problematic was the instruction we received in political theory or philosophy—which by then had become my main scholarly interest. The instruction was provided by a lively or spirited teacher who excelled in stimulating debate or controversy in the classroom—but a debate that was often fueled by strongly religious (and, as it seemed to me, fundamentalist) convictions. In his presentation, the entire history of Western modernity appeared as a downward slide from the heights reached in antiquity and the Middle Ages, a slide leading steadily into the morass of relativism and nihilism. Given my prior affection for Bobbio and my (limited) exposure to American pragmatism, this doctrine of decline—no matter how valuable as an antidote to the ideology of progress—was to me intellectually unappealing and unpersuasive. Thus, despite our shared focus on political philosophy, that teacher and I proceeded to go our separate ways—a fact that, no doubt, was due in part to my youthful age and a certain headstrong tendency in those years.

Surprisingly, the teacher who perhaps had the greatest influence on me at Duke was a man who taught American constitutional law with a focus on decisions of the American Supreme Court. His name was Robert Rankin, a native of North Carolina. Among all the fields of study, American constitutional law was newest to me and farthest removed from my previous experiences. In Rankin's review of successive court decisions, I was amazed by the subtlety of the arguments of justices, their attentiveness to earlier precedents coupled with a readiness to reinterpret past decisions in the light of concrete details and prevailing circumstances. Trained in the civil law tradition (with its preference for codified legal norms), I was stunned by the display of practical good judgment—what Aristotle called *phronesis*—on the part of justices and also by their interpretive skills (which gave me a foretaste of my later study of hermeneutics). Also, the division of court rulings into majority and minority opinions seemed to me indicative of an awareness that law is not a fixed, codifiable maxim but a living idea open to multiple (though not arbitrary) readings.

There was another aspect that drew me to Rankin as a teacher. My final year at Duke coincided with the beginning of the civil rights struggle, which brought turmoil to the still completely segregated American South. Although himself a Southerner, Robert Rankin at that time became a member of the U.S. Civil Rights Commission charged with the task of promoting racial equality throughout the country. As a member of that Commission, he had to travel to many Southern cities, holding hearings on prevailing abuses—and often requiring the protection of federal marshals against local threats or attacks. It was a great honor and privilege for me when, soon after my graduation in 1960, Rankin asked me to join him in writing a text on "emergency powers"—which became a book (my first) listing us both as joint authors.[30]

In the meantime, I had written and finally defended my doctoral dissertation under the joint guidance of Rankin and the teacher in comparative politics (Taylor Cole). The topic of my thesis was comparative on a philosophical or theoretical plane—something I much later would call comparative political theory. The specific focus of the thesis was on the idea or ideas of equality prevailing at the time of the American and French Revolutions. As it was clear to me, the idea of equality (or equal liberty) was one of the architectonic principles undergirding Western modernity; but its precise meaning was hazy and ill-defined. In the course of my study I discovered that there were several, principally two, distinct meanings of the term. One was the notion of a strict egalitarianism inspired by the rationalist strand of the Enlightenment and the scientific preference for quantitative measurement; the ultimate tendency of this strand was to construe equality as sameness or identity. Another conception was more qualitative and humanistic and aimed to promote primarily an equality of dignity or respect (in the midst of a tolerable range of differences). In a rough approximation one could say that the Jacobin spirit during the early phase of the French Revolution was wedded to a strict egalitarianism—involving the reduction of concrete cases to a universal rule—while the leaders of the American Revolution favored a more practical-qualitative approach. Although himself reared in the French Enlightenment, it was above all Montesquieu who anchored modern republican or democratic government in a pervasive "love of equality"—meaning by that phrase an ethical or humanitarian commitment. Apart from Montesquieu there was at the time a host of French and American thinkers giving to "equality" a plethora of nuanced meanings—a fact that ultimately made me shrink from transforming my thesis into a publishable study.[31]

PURDUE UNIVERSITY

When I graduated from Duke University in 1960, the job situation in the country was grim, leaving opportunities only for a limited number of graduates. Happily, Duke University decided to keep me on the teaching staff for another year. This was the year during which I coauthored with Robert Rankin the text mentioned before. It was also the year when the civil rights struggle was steadily gathering momentum, leading to many intense confrontations. Several of my classmates at Duke participated in lunch counter sit-ins and other forms of civil disobedience, and some were arrested; one of those arrested later brought court action under the emerging civil rights legislation and his case was litigated from the local courts all the way to the Supreme Court (where he was finally vindicated). Needless to say, my sympathies were strongly on the side of the demonstrators—although I had to proceed cautiously given my status as a "resident alien." After having applied to numerous colleges and universities, I finally secured a regular teaching position, starting in fall of 1961, at an institution in Milwaukee.

The institution was a college for women called Milwaukee Downer College—for me an entirely novel experience. Moving from a small town in the South, my wife and I enjoyed the rich cultural opportunities offered in the bigger city and also the location near Lake Michigan. The downside was my heavy teaching load: with only two people in the department, I had to teach virtually every subfield in the discipline of political science. To escape from this situation—and also because the college was undergoing radical restructuring—I went back on the market and was fortunate enough to receive an offer from a large state university: Purdue University in Indiana. My move

there in 1963 inaugurated for me a period that proved to be extremely beneficial in both intellectual and personal terms.

After the confining academic regimen in Milwaukee, Purdue University
offered a rich intellectual environment marked by genuine collegiality and a
pronounced hospitality for innovative ideas. By participating in periodic
interdisciplinary seminars or symposia, it was possible without great difficulty to become acquainted with the ongoing research agendas of colleagues in
cognate fields—above all the fields of literature, sociology, psychology, and
philosophy. Needless to say, interactions in seminars were soon continued
and extended in more informal settings, over meals or in private homes.
Although I was formally located in political science, my closest contacts
during the ensuing years developed with colleagues in philosophy (whose
offices were in the same building). These contacts prompted me to pursue
and deepen my philosophical interests. It so happens that Purdue University
was home to a number of distinguished philosophers specializing in recent
European philosophy, particularly phenomenology and existentialism. One
of these colleagues was an expert on Edmund Husserl (the founder of modern phenomenology) and his student Martin Heidegger; another colleague
had written on Karl Jaspers, while a third was well known for his interpretations of Jean-Paul Sartre. I had read these Continental thinkers before but
only sporadically, due to the demands placed on me by my legal and political
studies. Now I could delve into them with greater leisure, consulting both
their original texts and available English translations.

Perhaps the colleague who, in the long run, had the greatest impact on me
at Purdue was the phenomenologist and Heidegger scholar Calvin Schrag. In
discussions with him and in reading some of his books, I came to admire his
sure grasp of the spirit animating recent Continental philosophy, and especially his nuanced assessment of the relation between Husserl and his foremost student. Although some of his views did not immediately register with
me, they had a deep long-range effect. Above all, his scholarly and balanced
discussion of Heidegger's work helped to smooth my own access to that
thinker and to weaken my resistance to him. As I shall point out later, Heidegger had been a stumbling block for me for some time, mainly because of
his reputed politics and the strong accusations leveled against him by some
of my liberal friends. As a staunch Democrat, Schrag aroused in me some
early doubts about the accuracy of these accusations. The doubts were
strengthened by another circumstance: the fact that, in addition to being a
Heidegger scholar, Schrag was also fond of the theologian Paul Tillich,
whom he had met during his student days at Harvard. As it happens, some of
Tillich's key notions—like "Being," "Courage to Be," and "Ultimate Concern"—are very close to Heideggerian terminology (a fact due, at least in
part, to their meeting at Marburg University in the 1920s). Politically speaking, however, Tillich was a fierce opponent of Hitler and the Nazi regime,

emigrated to America in 1933, and beamed anti-Nazi messages from America to Germany throughout World War II. It occurred to me: if it was possible to draw such starkly divergent political lessons, then surely the totalizing indictment leveled against Heidegger by his opponents was not mandatory.[32]

Among his other activities, Schrag was also one of the founders of the Society for Phenomenology and Existential Philosophy (SPEP), a professional association that I joined early on (I believe in 1963) and whose annual meetings I would faithfully attend during subsequent decades. Participation in these meetings offered to me an intensive training in all the different facets of twentieth-century European philosophy: from phenomenology and existentialism to the later trends of structuralism, poststructuralism, and deconstruction. Most of the leading American experts in these fields gathered at these meetings—a great opportunity for me to discuss philosophical issues and, in due course, to become closely acquainted with them. I was fortunate in being able to interact for many years with such distinguished philosophers as John Sallis, William Richardson, Theodore Kisiel, John Caputo, Merold Westphal, and many others.[33] The only colleague from the field of political theory who regularly attended the meetings was the Korean-American Hwa Yol Jung, who soon became a close friend.[34] I should add that, a few years after its founding, SPEP was joined by a sister association called Society for Phenomenology and the Human Sciences (SPHS), which catered mostly to social scientists interested in Continental thought. A main focus of that society was on social phenomenologists like Alfred Schutz and social ethnomethodologists like Harold Garfinkel. The founder of the society, sociologist George Psathas, and many of its members became valuable allies for me in the struggle to humanize the social sciences. Psathas also created a new journal called *Human Studies* on whose editorial board I served for several decades.

Studying Continental thought became for me a consuming passion during my years at Purdue. Among all my readings what attracted me most was an outlook capable of finding a midpoint between "pure" or transcendental phenomenology and concrete or mundane affairs—something which has often been called existential phenomenology. As it appeared to me then (and still does), it was above all the French philosopher Maurice Merleau-Ponty who had articulated such a midpoint or middle path through his emphasis on the relational (as opposed to egocentric) character of human life and his linking of reason and affection or sensation.[35] There was another feature at Purdue which I appreciated because of its contribution to both intellectual and practical-interpersonal growth. Although largely dependent on state funding, the university had (and still has) a well-developed structure of academic self-government. Bringing together people from diverse academic fields, the Faculty Senate—on which I served for several years—was a place of open dialogue and debate that could serve as a model for public assemblies and the

Maurice Merleau-Ponty, French philosopher at Ecole Normale in Paris; photo: www.philosophical-investigations.org/Users/PerigGouanvic.

fostering of that public sphere so crucial for politics. Apart from participating in the Senate, I was involved in academic self-government on a more local level: by serving as chair of the Department of Political Science for five years—a position that taught me much about administrative matters and about the need to be responsive to individual colleagues while cultivating a sense of shared purpose. The university also offered me other opportunities, especially in the form of study-abroad programs. On a personal level, my nearly fifteen years at Purdue University brought the ultimate joy of family life: the birth of our two children, Dominique (1966) and Philip (1968), and the experience of the many marvels and surprises of parenting small children.

THE TWO CULTURES

Finding myself placed in the discipline of political science, one of my initial endeavors at Purdue was to gain greater clarity about the intellectual and epistemological location of this field in the academic context. For someone coming from Europe like me, political science was somewhat of a novelty, and perhaps an anomaly. On the one hand, the study of politics had traditionally been closely linked with ethics and law and thus loosely occupied a place among the humanities; on the other hand, modern science—in the sense of strict natural science methodology—had for some time made inroads into the social sciences and was getting ready to conquer the study of politics as well. I was dimly familiar with the conflict of academic faculties in the past, and especially with long discussions regarding the respective traits of the so-called *Naturwissenschaften* and *Geisteswissenschaften* (deriving from the Cartesian distinction between mind and external nature). But what were the implications of these disputes with regard to the study of politics? As it happens, the conflict between academic disciplines had been discussed in recent years by Lord Snow in a famous text titled *The Two Cultures* (first published in 1959). In this book, the respective characters and orientations of the natural and human sciences were clearly pinpointed, but in such a manner as to leave no room for mediation or a meeting ground. Subsequently, in a sequel titled *A Second Look*, Snow pondered precisely the possibility of such a meeting ground, which he termed "third culture" and which included the social and political disciplines. [36]

Intrigued and stimulated by Snow's initiative, I decided to explore the situation more closely on my own. One of my earliest published essays in America is in fact titled "Political Science and the Two Cultures." Going beyond Snow's account, I delved into the historical background of the struggle between academic disciplines, looking at arguments stretching from Vico and Kant to Wilhelm Dilthey, Heinrich Rickert, Wilhelm Windelband, and Max Weber. Moving forward into the actual practice of the study of politics, I focused both on the upsurge of scientific methodology (behaviorism) and attempts by practitioners to preserve the integrity of political study either in opposition to the behaviorist or positivist model or in the sense of a possible "third culture." Among strongly antipositivist works I paid attention especially to Eric Voegelin's *The New Science of Politics* (1952) and Friedrich Hayek's *The Counter-Revolution of Science* (1964), while also scrutinizing moves toward a possible third alternative among such writers as Peter Winch and Michael Oakeshott. Simultaneously, I was attracted to efforts to reformulate in a comprehensive sense the relation between academic disciplines, although the proper way to proceed was to me quite unclear. To some extent, Max Scheler's earlier proposal (of the 1920s) still seemed to me plausible when he distinguished between three types of knowledge or cognition (*Wis-*

sensformen): an inquiry dedicated to control of nature (*Leistungswissen*); an inquiry devoted to better understanding and practice (*Bildungswissen*); and an inquiring aiming at inner liberation and redemption (*Erlösungswissen*).[37] As it happened, this kind of proposal foreshadowed later initiatives by Frankfurt School theorists in this domain.

One thing that was reasonably clear was that the various approaches, whether humanist or not, were predicated on some "image of man," that is, some conception of the character of the participants in social and political life. Thus, some approaches—especially structural-functionalist or systems theories—assumed societies to be tightly organized along functional lines and accordingly defined social participants basically as pliant role players or performers of preordained scripts. On the other hand, individualistic approaches—especially exchange and rational choice theories—construed social life as a contractual arrangement and participants as private entrepreneurs and competitors. Finally, group-based approaches perceived social life basically as a clash between cultural, economic, or religious interests and participants as agents in the struggle for power. Looking around in the literature, it was not too difficult to discern and pinpoint the underlying anthropological conceptions or "images of man." Thus, in critiquing functionalist approaches, social theorist Ralf Dahrendorf had distilled as the guiding image that of the "role-player" and compliant social actor, whom he termed *homo sociologicus*. On the other hand, if the core of social and political life is seen as economic transaction, then individual actors are bound to have the character of utility maximizers congruent with the familiar image of *homo economicus*. In the case of conflict models, finally, the prototypical agent could be described as a power seeker or *homo politicus*, as that image was sketched in Harold Lasswell's influential study *Psychopathology and Politics*. The typical "political man," Lasswell stipulated, is a character "searching out the power institutions in society" and devoting all energies to "the capture and use of government."[38]

Explorations of these personality types led me progressively into the domain of philosophical anthropology, a field of inquiry enjoying considerable popularity at that time. As with regard to types of knowledge, the field had an important precursor in Max Scheler who, some decades ago, had sought to pinpoint the "position of man in the cosmos" by emphasizing the aspects of reflective consciousness and "spiritual" openness to the divine. After World War II, the main protagonists of philosophical anthropology in Germany were Arnold Gehlen, Erich Rothacker, and Helmuth Plessner. Among these writers, I felt most strongly attracted to Plessner, partly out of critical opposition to Gehlen whose strong animus against modernity and innovative human agency was to me unappealing.

For Gehlen, human beings were in essence biologically deficient creatures who had to compensate for their deficiency by relying on stable social structures and political institutions. By contrast, Plessner made room for human openness to new experiences and self-discovery through trial and error. Although not denying a certain kind of biological deficiency (by comparison with animals), he perceived in that feature a possible benefit in terms of greater human flexibility and distinctive cultural and artistic achievements. One of Plessner's central ideas was that of the "eccentric" position of human beings in the world, a position that places them at the cusp between nature and culture and also between convention and innovation. In this placement, I detected an important step beyond the Cartesian mind-matter bifurcation and beyond many similar dualisms besetting the modern age. Very dimly, I also perceived here a possible parallel with Martin Heidegger's notion of the "ek-centric" status of *Dasein* as well as a parallel with the kind of critical anthropology developed at the time by Frankfurt School theorists.[39]

Like Scheler before him, Plessner saw himself as standing in the tradition of modern phenomenology as initiated by Edmund Husserl. In tandem with my study of philosophical anthropology I found myself steadily drawn to that tradition. What attracted me initially above all was Husserl's break with abstract philosophical reasoning and his bold admonition to turn "to the things themselves" (*zu den Sachen selbst*). This call seemed akin to the move of modern Western painters from closeted studios to outdoor painting animated by the desire to see phenomena with fresh eyes. Delving into the rich diversity of the phenomenological movement, I became aware of certain limitations of Husserl's approach, especially his preoccupation with "transcendental idealism"—limitations that prompted many of his followers to branch out in new directions. As mentioned before, I became attracted especially to French existential phenomenology. Due to my location in one of the human sciences, however, I also developed a strong interest in "social phenomenology" or "mundane phenomenology" in its different versions. The chief focus of this inquiry was on what Husserl had called the "life-world," a notion that now was given concrete social and even political connotations. As I came to see, the leading and most influential practitioner of social phenomenology was Alfred Schutz, the student of Husserl and Max Weber. In his *Phenomenology of the Social World* (1967), he employed Husserl's method in order to discern the intended meaning structures of the lived social world (*Umwelt*); adding a temporal dimension to this notion, he further differentiated between the worlds of contemporaries, predecessors, and successors (*Mitwelt, Vorwelt, Folgewelt*).[40]

My study of Alfred Schutz made clear to me the affinity between phenomenology and Max Weber's work, especially the latter's conception of "understanding" (*Verstehen*). Actually, starting from Weber's work, it was possible to trace a clear line leading from his conception via Ludwig Wittgenstein and Peter Winch to social phenomenology, ethnomethodology, all the way to hermeneutics and (a version of) "critical theory." It so happened that I frequently had to teach courses dealing with "scope and methods" or "scope and approaches" in the discipline. To my frustration, no good text-book was available for this purpose. In a conversation with Thomas McCarthy—who at the time was teaching philosophy at Boston University—I discovered that he was teaching similar courses and was similarly frustrat-ed. We decided to collaborate and to assemble in a text reading materials covering the broad range of cognate approaches—a text subsequently pub-lished under the title *Understanding and Social Inquiry.*[41] In addition to linking our research agendas, this collaboration established the basis for a lifelong friendship, which continued despite later moves in different direc-tions.

POLITICAL THEORY AND THE COLD WAR

My chief teaching obligations at Purdue University were in the field of political theory or philosophy. Hence, my years there involved my introduc-tion into a larger professional community specializing in that field. As a relative newcomer I was struck by the sheer size and diversity of this profes-sional community. Compared with the situation in other countries, the com-munity seemed marked by intellectual vibrancy and intense individual rival-ries. No doubt, I owe a considerable debt to this vibrancy and to the work of many colleagues in the field. Nevertheless, coming from my background, I could not help being surprised or taken aback by some peculiar aspects. As practiced in the United States, political theory tended to be almost entirely separated from the discipline of philosophy. Hence, practitioners would fo-cus on narrowly "political" texts of philosophers while leaving aside their more theoretical works. Thus, while highlighting Plato's *Republic* and *Laws*, little attention is given to his metaphysical dialogues; similarly, while center-staging John Locke's *Treatises of Civil Government*, one seems dispensed from studying his *Essay Concerning Human Understanding*. Given a pre-sumed lack of political insights, Descartes is almost entirely ignored; so is Kant's first *Critique*.

Undoubtedly, some of the blame for this divorce must rest on the shoul-ders of professional philosophy. By privileging such trends as logical positi-vism and conceptual analysis, American philosophy in mid-century had in a way exiled itself from politics and ethics while seeking shelter behind the safe walls of technical expertise. However, part of the blame must also be shared by political theorists for retreating into a parallel professionalism and academic careerism—safe from the inroads not only of other disciplines (including economics, sociology, psychology, and anthropology) but also the contagion of public life. As a result of this retreat, political theory often appears as the province of a gated community, as an ingrown and purely historicist enterprise involving the celebration of past canons at the expense of forward-looking vistas and broader social engagements.

To be sure, even when officially shunned, politics has a way of asserting itself, if only as an amorphous climate or *Zeitgeist*. During the time of my stay at Purdue, the dominant *Zeitgeist* was the Cold War. Most American intellectuals, including political theorists, defined their position in one way or other with reference to the Cold War. Even seemingly recondite thinkers, preoccupied mainly with antiquity or the Middle Ages, at crucial junctures displayed the imprint of this confrontation. Basically, for intellectuals in the West, echoing the *Zeitgeist* meant to be ardently opposed to all kinds of collectivism—not only communism and Soviet-style Marxism but also milder forms of socialism and social experimentation. Under the auspices of this mentality, the West came to define itself as the "Free World," with freedom meaning chiefly "negative freedom," that is, liberty *from* social and political commitments and constraints. However, something curious happened to liberalism during these years. Seeing that, in earlier times, liberalism had often encouraged forms of social experimentation, a terminological confusion ensued in the sense that the term "liberal" (although ostensibly deriving from "liberty") became suspect in the West. The confusion was deepened by the valorization of "liberal" laissez-faire economics alongside the downgrading of social and political progressivism.

As stated before, the Cold War deeply penetrated into the academy, often encouraging ideological rigidity. The latter tendency was further strengthened by the development of various schools of thought initially inspired by strong intellectual personalities but subsequently, among their followers, turning into sectarian movements with strong restorative tendencies. During the decades after World War II, American political theory was strongly influenced by two immigrant intellectuals: Leo Strauss and Eric Voegelin. No doubt, both were eminently learned scholars and writers; in terms of the *Zeitgeist*, however, both located themselves—or were located by their followers—on one side of the Cold War divide. Both were dismayed by certain aspects of Western modernity and modern liberalism, and especially by the temptation of liberalism to slide toward either socialism or anarchism. During my years at Purdue, I came to know both thinkers, although I never joined the coterie of their followers. In the case of Strauss, I appreciated his intellectual discipline and his insistence on close textual reading (as an antidote to the shallow glosses often favored by political theorists). However, I did not share his fascination with esoteric reading and writing nor his focus on a presumed authorial intent (that is, the attempt to read the author's mind). I applauded his attempt to revive the classics and especially Platonic thought but found him insufficiently attentive to the "zetetic" or searching quality of Socratic questioning (and hence vulnerable to charges of Platonic essentialism). I was also impressed by the broad sweep of his historical erudition but was unable to accept his portrayal of modern Western thought as nothing but a downhill slide (from Machiavelli to Hobbes and Rousseau to nihilism).[42]

In the prevailing context, the two thinkers contributed in subtle ways to a certain shift in America from liberalism to conservatism (and neoconservatism), although they certainly cannot be blamed for the excesses that arose after they passed away.[43] In the case of Voegelin, I appreciated again his scholarship and historical erudition but was unable to accept his reduction of modern political thought to a form of "gnosticism" nor his assignment of a foundational role to the somewhat obscure medieval figure of Joachim of Fiore. In the same context, I found his portrayal of Hegel as an intellectual "sorcerer" ill-conceived and untenable. One of the things I found appealing was Voegelin's willingness to reconcile philosophical reason and faith, *logos* and *mythos* (resonating distantly with the Erasmian motto of *fides et eruditio*). Another appealing feature for me was his partial attention to Continental phenomenology, evident in his reflections on the role of "consciousness" and in his correspondence with Alfred Schutz. What I found missing, however, was a willingness to move forward with this perspective in new directions, as illustrated in the following episode: During the time I served as chair of political science at Purdue University, I invited Voegelin for a lecture. Before his talk I met with him for discussion in my office, which was lined with many shelves of book. Looking around, he detected a shelf lined with German books published by the avant-garde Suhrkamp Verlag in Frankfurt— which elicited his comment that I had too many "wrong books."[44]

My relation to these thinkers was marked also by a generational difference. Trying to find my own way during these years, I felt myself increasingly drawn to an amorphous set of younger theorists who, like me, were chiefly preoccupied with contemporary issues. Using a broad label, most of these theorists were progressive in some way, although the term had become ambivalent and contested by that time. Without exhibiting a "school" spirit, most of the members in the group were indebted to, or influenced by, a prominent senior scholar named Sheldon Wolin. Apart from a number of other writings, Wolin had made his mark through a book titled *Politics and Vision*, which by contrast to many restorative texts, stressed the forward-looking or visionary character of political thought.[45] Crudely phrased, *vision* here meant a strengthening of some kind of liberal and social democracy, in opposition to both Soviet collectivism and reactionary (or fascist) tendencies. Although inspired in some fashion by Wolin's work, the theorists with whom I associated were free of sectarian leanings and pursued very different lines of inquiry. For some, liberalism meant a strengthening of social welfare programs, while for others it favored "negative liberty" and a retreat into, or cultivation of, private inwardness. Given this diversity, it was natural that I should be drawn more closely to some among them than to others. The colleague whose work I came to appreciate particularly during these years was William Connolly, a thinker who, without neglecting the history of political thought, was able to rescue political theory from the "rearview mirror" and to orient it toward an engagement with contemporary intellectual and political experiences.[46]

During the ensuing years, my relation with Connolly and his circle of friends deepened, despite greatly changing circumstances. The events of 1968, in particular, gave a powerful boost to innovative or progressive political thinking; so did the intense controversy surrounding the Vietnam War. As is well known, of course, the same events triggered an intense backlash or counter-move, a move that later fueled the upsurge of a fervent right-wing agenda (labeled "neoconservatism"). On the whole, these developments involved an intensification of the prevailing Cold War mentality and further threw into disarray traditional political terminology, including the meaning of "liberalism." Among questions urgently surfacing were these: Was it the task of "liberals" to export (American-style) liberty around the world, if necessary by force of arms? And was the cherished liberty identical with the pursuit of private self-interest, or else with the promotion of broader social programs? For me, coming from my background, the Cold War *Zeitgeist* seemed unappealing and intellectually debilitating. Given my interest in phenomenology, including French phenomenology, I was familiar with Merleau-Ponty's text *Humanism and Terror* (1947) in which he castigated the Cold War antithesis between a presumably benign Western liberalism and the "terrorism" of Soviet collectivism. "It is the essence of liberty," he wrote there, "to exist only in the practice of liberty, in the inevitably imperfect movement which joins us to others, to the things of the world, to our jobs, mixed with the hazard of our situation." This insight offered to me a possible exit route beyond polarized political agendas.[47]

GADAMER AND HABERMAS

One of the distinct benefits of my years at Purdue was the opportunity to participate in study abroad programs in different parts of the world. One such program, maintained by Purdue jointly with Indiana University, was located in Hamburg, Germany, and permitted students (with some proficiency in the language) to attend classes at Hamburg University. Annually a group of about twenty-five students from both institutions would spend two semesters in Hamburg under the guidance of a program director and some adjunct faculty. It so happened that I was appointed program director for the period from fall 1968 through summer 1969. The year proved to be very fruitful and also filled with unexpected excitement. Having been raised in Southern Germany, I found life in cosmopolitan Hamburg extremely enjoyable, especially after having spent many years in small American college towns. Life was made particularly pleasant by the presence of my wife and our two young children (ages three and one) and also by the fact that the program provided us with a large, centrally located apartment. During the fall of 1968 I became acquainted with several colleagues at Hamburg University who proceeded to invite me to teach courses there during the following spring and summer semester. This was the beginning of a close relationship with that university that lasted for many years and led to repeated teaching engagements (in 1971–72, 1976, and 1986). In this manner I was able to observe German university life from the inside and to experience both its strengths and weakness over a period of time.[48]

As indicated before, 1968 was not just any ordinary year. In many ways, it was a political as well as intellectual watershed. Politically, opposition to the Vietnam war dramatically gathered momentum both in America and in Europe. Most forcefully, this opposition found expression in the upsurge of the student movement or New Left movement, an upsurge leading to large-scale demonstrations in many parts of the Western world. Simultaneously, the near-collapse of the French government in that year triggered an intellectual sea-change in Europe, a change that—setting itself off against the existentialist humanism of the postwar years—inaugurated a trend which came to be known as "postmodernism" and "poststructuralism" (and in due course achieved prominence in America as well). A large city with a sizeable student population, Hamburg was quickly drawn into the maelstrom of these events. Student demonstrations became a steady feature of city life; for several months, students even occupied the main administrative building of the university (a high-rise known as the *Philosophenturm* or "philosophers' tower"), though without significantly disrupting lectures or seminars. Several prominent intellectuals visited Hamburg and addressed large gatherings; among these intellectuals was a professor from Frankfurt named Jürgen Habermas. I had heard about him and had read some of his early publications. In the turbulent political scene at the time, Habermas was a figure providing inspiration as well as orientation: although in sympathy with many of the students' demands, he also cautioned them against excesses that would tarnish their cause. Impressed by his stance I asked some of my Hamburg colleagues to introduce me to him, which they did. This was the beginning of a friendly relationship between Habermas and myself that lasted for several decades (and in one sense never came to an end).

During the ensuing years, several factors conspired to deepen this friendly relationship. It so happened that during 1968 Habermas published a book on the nature of social inquiry under the title *Erkenntnis und Interesse* (later translated as *Knowledge and Human Interests*).[49] The book greatly impressed me, mainly for two reasons: it contested and broke with the positivist claim to monopolize social knowledge; at the same time, it reaffirmed a linkage between different forms of knowledge and corresponding human

Juergen Habermas, philosopher/sociologist at the University of Frankfurt; Arne Dedert/Alamy Stock Photo.

motivations or interests (and hence between thought and practice). In his study, Habermas distinguished between three chief motivations—technical control, practical understanding, and emancipation—undergirding respectively the endeavors of science, hermeneutics, and self-reflection (a distinction distantly recalling Max Scheler's *Wissensformen*). After my return to America, I presented a paper at a professional meeting in New York in which I discussed Habermas's work, with a focus on his tripartite epistemology. To my knowledge, this was the first time that his work was highlighted at a professional gathering in America.[50] Subsequently, Habermas asked me to edit a German-language volume assembling some of the major responses to his epistemological book, which I did under the title *Materialienband zu Erkenntnis und Interesse*.[51] Our initial contacts were strengthened by encounters at numerous conferences both in Germany and in America and by visits to our respective homes. At the time when I served as chair at Purdue University, I invited him for a lecture, which was attended by a large audience. Still somewhat later I assembled together with philosopher Seyla Benhabib another reader or *Materialienband*, on what Habermas had come to call his "discourse ethics" or "communicative ethics."[52]

When in Hamburg, I also become interested in the work of the philosopher Hans-Georg Gadamer whose major book, *Truth and Method*, had been published a few years earlier.[53] During a lull in my university schedule, I decided to travel to Southern Germany and especially to Heidelberg where Gadamer was teaching. Traveling by train I arrived in Heidelberg in the early afternoon. After checking into a small hotel I ventured out to explore the city and the university. Great was my surprise when I came into the streets surrounding the university: red flags were hanging out of many windows and graffiti covered many walls. I was told that the student movement had taken over and now occupied the entire university. Somewhat downcast because I wouldn't be able to see Gadamer, I went into a restaurant for a meal. On my table I was joined by a young man who turned out to be a student. He told me that the university was closed and that all lectures had been canceled. Hearing this I became even more distressed. Noticing my chagrin, the young man asked me for the reason, and I told him that I had come from Hamburg to see Gadamer. At this point, his eyes lighted up and he told me that I was in luck: the only lectures and seminars not canceled were those given by Gadamer. He also told me that a lecture course was offered that very evening in a building near the river called the *Heustadel,* which I could attend.

Needless to say, I was overjoyed. After finishing my meal, I went looking for the building the student had described. Here another real surprise awaited me: on entering the building, the noise and turbulence of the city suddenly vanished. The lecture hall was quiet and peaceful, with many students sitting at their desks reading and obviously preparing themselves for the lecture. At the announced time, Professor Gadamer entered the room together with an assistant. Without wasting any time, he immediately started with a question (which I recall vividly): "Was ist Wesen? Was ist das Wesentliche?" (What is essence and the essential?) The lecture—which lasted for almost two hours—dealt with Edmund Husserl's transcendental phenomenology and his effort to grasp the essential meaning of phenomena. I was greatly struck by Gadamer's lucid exposition, by his determined concentration on the *Sache,* the topic under investigation. Arguments that, when read on paper, seemed obscure and perhaps impenetrable, suddenly appeared readily accessible and nearly transparent. Following a question period, the session ended and Gadamer was ready to depart. At this point I marshalled my courage and introduced myself to him. He was very friendly, especially when noting that I had traveled some distance just to see him. I told him that the lecture hall served like an island, an oasis of reflection, in the midst of a brewing storm. With a smile he invited me to come to a seminar he was going to conduct the following day at another place; that time the topic was going to be Martin Heidegger who I knew was his foremost teacher.

The seminar I attended the next day was again surprising by its calm atmosphere. Intellectually, the experience was perhaps even more impressive than the previous lecture. Conducted in dialogical fashion and lasting for nearly three hours, the seminar dealt with Heidegger's *Letter on Human-*

Hans-Georg Gadamer, philosopher at the University of Heidelberg; dpa picture alliance/Alamy Stock Photo.

ism.[54] The intensity of the focus on the *Sache* was stunning: during the entire period of the seminar, we managed to discuss barely three or four sentences of the *Letter*. Under Gadamer's guidance, however, these few sentences served as gateways to Heidegger's entire philosophy, as passkeys to the sprawling edifice of his thought. After the seminar, I expressed my appreciation to him and my eagerness to study his writings still more closely.[55] As it turned out, this visit to Heidelberg was the beginning of a friendly relationship that lasted without interruptions until his death.

Our meeting there was followed by many subsequent encounters, at conferences, large and small gatherings, and visits to each other's homes. When I was chair at Purdue University, I invited him for a public lecture and once to a symposium together with Habermas and Karl-Otto Apel. As mentioned before, I returned to Hamburg repeatedly as a visiting professor. It so happened that one of Gadamer's close students, Rainer Wiehl, was during that time teaching in Hamburg; in response to Wiehl's invitation, he would come to the city for lectures—which were often followed by leisurely discussions in Wiehl's large garden at his home near the Elbe river. Still later, I participated for many years in summer seminars organized by a group of Gadamer's followers in Heidelberg, seminars in which he would participate regularly despite his advancing years. Since our meetings were held in the philosophical institute at the university, our papers were presented under the watchful eyes not only of Gadamer but also of Hegel, whose imposing bust stood in the corner. The high point of our summer meetings would come at the end when Gadamer invariably would invite us to dinner in a lovely restaurant at the Neckar River. On these occasions, I came to appreciate fully his urbane spirit and his genuine fondness for conviviality. [56]

Having become acquainted with both Habermas and Gadamer in the same year, I was in a quandary: I was attracted to both but also realized that there was a difference with which I would have to deal at some point. The need to clarify matters imposed itself soon enough. As it happens, the following decade (the 1970s) was intellectually overshadowed by a dispute that, though originating on the Continent, quickly came to affect North American discussions: the so-called Habermas-Gadamer debate. Broadly speaking, the debate pitted Habermas's critical theory against Gadamer's hermeneutics *cum* phenomenology—or, to simplify and localize matters, Frankfurt versus Freiburg. The debate was initiated by Habermas's extensive review of Gadamer's *Truth and Method* published in a leading philosophical journal. [57] Although praising the scope of Gadamer's work and the depth of some of its insights, Habermas took exception chiefly to the claimed universality of hermeneutics, the claim that interpretive understanding undergirds all forms of human knowledge or cognitive pursuits. Against this argument, Habermas marshaled his own tripartite scheme, which he had recently articulated: the division between empirical knowledge, hermeneutics, and self-understanding. In his account, this tripartition was better able to recognize the role of empirical science and also made room for "critique" in the sense of a critical dismantling of self-delusions (facilitated by Freudian depth psychology).

In a response to this review, Gadamer for his part expressed appreciation for the reviewer's diligence but also drew some important lines of demarcation. Regarding empirical science, he was quite ready to acknowledge its importance in modern life—but not its independence from interpretative understanding. By relying precisely on the pragmatic "community of investigators" invoked by Habermas, he was able to show the indispensable role of interpretation (a point reinforced more recently by the upsurge of postempiricist epistemology). With regard to critical self-understanding, Gadamer challenged the parallel drawn by Habermas between individual psychic therapy and social liberation or emancipation, arguing forcefully that society with all its ills was not a "patient" amenable to therapy administered by the critical theorist.

The debate continued in a series of rejoinders and counter-rejoinders. In the course of these exchanges, Habermas withdrew some of his initial claims while upholding and even reinforcing others. The claim he most quickly withdrew was the parallel between individual-psychic and social liberation, replacing this parallel in due course with borrowings from Jean Piaget's developmental cognitive psychology. One of the more surprising modifications was his willingness to loosen if not to abandon the linkage between knowledge and interests, or between theory and practical motivations (a change that seemed to be a concession less to Gadamer than to cognitive rationalism and the steady inroads of American analytical philosophy). With these changes, the original tripartite epistemology was left in place—still confronted with Gadamer's original view of a universal hermeneutics.

There is no need here to recount in detail the different phases of the debate, something which has repeatedly been done in the literature.[58] Eventually, the debate petered out, being overtaken by new intellectual developments (especially the rise of postmodernism). For me personally, however, the debate was not only of abstractly theoretical but also of existential significance. Having been drawn to both Habermas and Gadamer, I felt that I was torn both intellectually and existentially. Was there perhaps the possibility of reconciling the differences, by giving to each position its due? For some time, I persuaded myself that the tension was actually fruitful and productive. In some publications, I placed myself deliberately between the two positions, that is, figuratively "between Frankfurt and Freiburg."[59] Over time, however, I became uncomfortable with this stance, which seemed to involve no more than the effort to "split the difference."[60]

Several factors contributed to my increasing discomfort. One factor was my growing appreciation of the strength of Gadamer's position, especially his claim of the general or universal scope of hermeneutics. This claim was buttressed, in my view, by the emphasis placed in recent philosophy of science on interpretive paradigms or frames of significance. Compared with this broad hermeneutical scope, Habermas's tripartite scheme—quite apart from unduly privileging epistemology—seemed to split cognitive endeavors apart in violation of their contiguity or continuity. The stress on self-emancipation, in particular, appeared predicated on the critical theorist's aloofness from interpretive contexts as such. This aloofness or distance was intensified by some Habermasian moves in the later phases of the debate.

One such move was to sever the linkage between knowledge and interests or between theory and practice. This move was soon followed by a more thorough decontextualization: the tendency to privilege universal reason or universal validity claims over any cultural or linguistic frames of reference—a tendency evident both in his revised theory of knowledge and his "discourse ethics" focused on universal norms (or "ought"-claims).[61] From my perspective, this privileging seemed to undermine or disrupt the calibrated balance between reason and experience favored by both pragmatism and existential phenomenology (and especially by Merleau-Ponty). The final discomforting factor was a basic philosophical lacuna: the failure of critical theory to raise the question of "being"—the "being" of humans and nature, of "is" and "ought"—a question which famously has been rekindled in recent times by Martin Heidegger. Given that the latter was a philosopher very close to Gadamer but entirely rejected by Habermas, it became clear to me that, at least in this respect, "splitting the difference" was not a possibility.

MARTIN HEIDEGGER

As I have mentioned before, my approach to Heidegger was slow and diffi-cult. I had sporadically read bits of his writings and caught additional glimpses through the intermediary of other writers (like Merleau-Ponty, Jean-Paul Sartre, and others). However, for quite some time, I was hesitant or reluctant to enter his world of thought, mainly for two reasons. One was philosophical: I did not quite find an entry to his thought, a passkey that would allow me to gain my bearings in his very complex writings. The other reason was strictly political: as an emigrant from Germany I did not know how to surmount the barrier erected by some of Heidegger's actions and pronouncements in 1933 and the early period of the Nazi regime. Since in a way this was a past I wanted to get away from, I was not eager to engage with a work connected with that past, although I realized that this work was much broader than the particular Nazi episode. My reluctance was powerful-ly supported by the strong anti-Heideggerian sentiments nurtured by many liberal intellectuals, including intellectuals (like Habermas) with whom I was on good terms. The opposition was sometimes so virulent and relentless that Heidegger's entire work was engulfed in the same political verdict (of fas-cism), just as his person was demeaned to the point of being nearly demon-ized. Although not overly timid by nature, I realized that I had to tread carefully in this field so as not to lose the good will of people I otherwise valued.

Hence my stance of deliberate distance—which, however, I could not maintain indefinitely. For one thing, there were German thinkers—like Gad-amer, Otto Pöggler, and Walter Biemel—who, as his students, were close to Heidegger and yet were free of the political stain mentioned before. (The same was true, as I mentioned, of Paul Tillich.) For another thing, I was viscerally opposed to literary censorship—and it seemed to me increasingly that Heidegger had been placed by many liberal thinkers on an index of forbidden books. As with the case of all forbidden books, my curiosity was stimulated. As it happened, one day almost absent-mindedly I opened one of Heidegger's books and was struck by the fact that he seemed to address precisely the questions that troubled me (and for which I had found little guidance in other contemporary texts). One of them was precisely the ques-tion of "being"—which was routinely bracketed by neo-Kantian thinkers as

Martin Heidegger, philosopher at the University of Freiburg; Really Easy Star/ Alamy Stock Photo.

well as most critical theorists. But how could this question be bracketed? Was it not indeed a legitimate and even urgent question to ask in which way different beings "are" and have being—tables, dogs, humans, ethical norms, and perhaps even gods? As Heidegger noted, it was this question that Aristotle had initially launched and that had enabled him to see all "beings," despite their manifold differences, as linked in some kind of continuity or contiguity. But as Heidegger also observed, in opposition to traditional formulations, being could no longer be grasped as a substance or fixed concept but needed to be seen as a temporal process or happening, an ongoing "disclosure" (and sheltering) of meaning in which all beings participate. Since my own being or *Dasein* is involved in this happening, how can I avoid asking about being? How can my own being be bracketed as a question?

Seeing that Heidegger's work addressed me so directly, I could not help but take up the challenge and immerse myself more deeply in his writings. Apart from the question of being, what impressed and struck me most forcefully was his critique of modern Western metaphysics, especially Cartesian rationalism with its focus on the *cogito*. As he pointed out persuasively, this focus was at the root of a profound split troubling modern life: the split between mind and matter, humans and the world, a rift associated with a host of other bifurcations such as those between subject and object, self and other, human beings and nature. By defining human existence as "being-in-the-world," Heidegger's work undercut these divisions in such a way as to make "world" in its many dimensions a constitutive feature of existence as such.[62] In my own work as a political theorist, these changes had a profound effect by unsettling some of the basic presumptions of modern political thought. Among these presumptions was the notion of a pre-social "state of nature" inhabited by isolated egos, coupled with the idea of a contractual origin of society and political regimes. In trying to come to terms with the demise of Cartesianism, I found myself confronted with a number of questions, especially these: What is the status of individualism and of traditional Western humanism? How should one construe the relation between self and other human beings, bypassing the options of contractual agreement and simple rational convergence? How was it possible to rethink the relation between humans and nature, once "nature" could no longer be simply externalized or objectified? What is the nature of history and social evolution, when agency is no longer anchored in intentional design? And finally, what is the role of language and communication in social life?

On all these questions I found Heidegger's initiatives deeply stimulating—especially when combined with arguments culled from Merleau-Ponty as well as writers of the early Frankfurt School (particularly Theodor Adorno). Some of my books written during this time give evidence of the intellectual ferment triggered by the questions mentioned above. My text *Twilight of Subjectivity* (1981), in particular, placed itself on the cusp between the older metaphysical paradigm rooted in individual subjectivity and the emerging outlook emphasizing human connectedness anchored in (Heideggerian) "care" and "solicitude."[63] It so happened that, during the ensuing years, several larger texts were released that Heidegger had penned in the 1930s, that is, during the heyday of the Nazi regime. Studying these texts, it became evident to me that, during these years, Heidegger underwent a profound *Kehre* or "turning" not only in a strictly philosophical but also a political sense.[64] As I discovered, several portions of these texts were not only covertly or indirectly but openly and directly critical of central tenets of National Socialist ideology (such as its racism, chauvinism, and "leadership" principle). In fact, I became increasingly convinced that Heidegger's philosophy is not only critical of but the very antithesis of this ideology. At this point, as my conviction grew, I would have dearly loved to visit and talk with Heidegger in his home in Frieburg, but he passed away (in 1976) before I could implement this plan. This is one of the regrets in my life: that the courage which had led me to visit other thinkers faltered in this instance.[65]

OXFORD AND POSTMODERNISM

In 1978, after having spent five years as department chair, I left Purdue in order to join the University of Notre Dame as an endowed professor. The university was then under the presidential guidance of Father Theodore Hesburgh who, by then, had acquired a national and international reputation. As previously mentioned, I had known about him through my teacher at Duke University, Robert Rankin, who had served with him on the U.S. Civil Rights Commission during the difficult period of the civil rights struggle. In addition to his years on that commission, Hesburgh was widely known for his active engagement in public life, especially for his service on a series of atomic energy, disarmament, and peace-making agencies. His most outstanding and appealing quality, from my point of view, was his combination of genuine religiosity with world-openness and commitment to social justice. In a way, I discovered in him again that broadly balanced Erasmian spirit that had guided me since my school days. During my interviews at the university, Father Hesburgh—in the course of a longer conversation—asked me whether I would be comfortable teaching at a Catholic university. Phrased in this manner, I could only answer the question affirmatively.

I formally joined Notre Dame in 1978, but I was on a leave of absence during the first year. I had received a research fellowship for that year from the National Endowment for the Humanities. Since, at that juncture, I was deeply interested in language and linguistic philosophy, I decided to spent the year in Oxford, England, which had a reputation for being a center of language studies—a lingering aura of the earlier era of Ludwig Wittgenstein. Culturally, Oxford proved to be a very pleasant and even exciting place. There were numerous small playhouses in which one could savor the gems of British and European drama. There was also an abundance of musical recitals, performed either in churches or some of the numerous colleges in the city. It was there that I first discovered some of the great British Renaissance composers whom I had not really known before—people like William Byrd and Thomas Tallis. In terms of my main philosophical interest, however, the place was a thorough disappointment. As I learned to my dismay, little or nothing of the Wittgensteinian legacy survived in Oxford (and the same was true to a lesser extent in nearby Cambridge). Among professors and philo-

U.S. Civil Rights Commission: Rev. Theodore M. Hesburgh, Robert Rankin, and Berl Bernhard talking with a group in Arizona (1962). Courtesy of University of Notre Dame Archives.

sophically interested students, discussions invariably centered on the works of Michael Dummet and Donald Davidson—analytical thinkers far removed from the concerns of a Continental humanist and existential phenomenologist. In terms of my stipend, I was housed as a Fellow in Nuffield College—a college catering mainly to empirical or quantitative social scientists with little or no interest in theory or philosophy.

Fortunately for me, Oxford—like most university towns—was not entirely one-dimensional and had a number of intellectually rewarding sides. One philosopher whom I valued highly from earlier readings was Stuart Hampshire who, in a way, upheld the humanist tradition against narrowly analytical trends. I attended some of his classes and was greatly impressed by his verve and lucidity, but I did not pursue the contact in the direction of a closer acquaintance.[66] Another teacher—actually a political philosopher—whom I came to know somewhat better during this time was Steven Lukes. He was teaching then at Balliol College, and I remember some of the lively discussions we had in his office about freedom and power, liberalism and socialism. The most redeeming quality of Oxford, however, from my vantage point was the presence of the Canadian philosopher and political theorist Charles Taylor. During that period, Taylor was staying at All Souls College and was offering seminars and lecture courses both in that college and for the larger university community. I had met him earlier at some conferences and had studied his writings with considerable interest. His work on Hegel and also his plea for an interpretive (or hermeneutical) mode of social inquiry were deeply congenial to me. Our common stay in Oxford gave me the welcome opportunity to deepen our earlier passing acquaintance into a closer relationship—a bond that remained firm during subsequent years.[67] Curiously, it was also during these Oxford days that a certain divergence between our perspectives came into view.

My stay in Oxford happened precisely a decade after the events of 1968. During the intervening years, the new philosophical orientation of postmodernism (also called poststructuralism) had emerged on the European continent. In its basic intent, the label signaled a break or rupture with some of the guiding linchpins of Western modernity—especially the centrality of the *cogito*, the subject-object split, and the reduction of nature to a target of technological control. Most of the postmodern thinkers were French; among them, Jean-François Lyotard, Jacques Derrida, Michel Foucault, and Gilles Deleuze had acquired considerable influence in Europe and incipiently in the United States—but not in England.[68] Confronted with the onslaught of the new philosophical genre, British analytical philosophy had circled the wagons and entrenched itself in staunch insularity. Being raised in the Continental tradition, the new postmodern trend was to me immediately and intuitively appealing whereas British insularity struck me as stifling and claustrophobic. To a Canadian like Charles Taylor, I discovered, the new trend was not appealing in the same way (in part, it seems, because of his strong mooring in German idealist philosophy).

Being intensely frustrated and stifled by the British scene, I desperately hankered for relief or a breath of fresh air—a breath, I thought, I could only find in France. The French writers who attracted me most at the time were Derrida and Foucault. In a string of writings, Derrida had carried forward some of Heidegger's philosophical initiatives, while also adding new layers of linguistic and literary subtlety. On the other hand, Foucault had retrieved some of the philosophically and politically unsettling aspects of Nietzsche's work, while also giving fresh impulses to postempiricist epistemology.[69] Full of eagerness, I wrote letters to both thinkers in Paris, expressing my desire to meet with them—and expecting to be disappointed. Great was my surprise when, in a week's time, both thinkers responded positively, inviting me to see them in Paris.

This was the beginning of my serious engagement with recent postmodern French thought. As soon as I could make the necessary arrangements, I traveled by train and boat to Paris. I recall the delight I felt when landing once again on the Continent where the air seemed saturated with intellectual daring and innovation. I myself was intellectually in some turmoil at the time. As indicated before, I was deeply troubled by, and alienated from, central pillars of Western modernity, especially the Cartesian legacy of the *cogito*. I felt a real urgency to break through these confines—but how? How to break free of the profound subject-centeredness endemic to modern Western life and thought? In a way, I found myself in the midst of a transition or transformation, perhaps on the brink of something like a *Kehre*. I mention this in order to explain my openness and receptivity to French thought. To be sure, the receptivity was never entirely uncritical; but at least initially, critical impulses were muffled or subdued in favor of the venture of a new "disclosure." As it seems to me now, Nietzsche's "new seas" and Heideggerian "ekstasis" were ready to dislodge me from familiar moorings and entice me to uncanny explorations beyond the poles of inside/outside, self/other, mine and yours. I felt eager to plumb the emptiness beyond all plenitude, the non-being beyond or alongside being, and the non-ego in the midst of ordinary sociality.

The first to respond to my letters was Jacques Derrida, and so I visited him first. He had invited me to see him in his office in the Ecole Normale. Remembering the many famous people who either studied or taught at that school, I felt intimidated. However, my timidity quickly vanished when, on entering his office, Derrida warmly welcomed me and shook my hand. (I had not received such a welcome from dons in Oxford.) He asked me about my background, my earlier studies, and my present occupation. On learning of my strong interest in political philosophy, he commented that Continental phenomenology had not sufficiently paid attention to that topic. The conversation shifted quickly to the issues that had actually brought me to his office: his relation to Husserl and Heidegger and his notion of "deconstruction." Regarding the former relation, Derrida observed that he had in general followed Heidegger's transformation or radicalization of Husserl's transcendental approach but added that, in his view, a further radical-

Jacques Derrida, Professor at the Ecole Normale in Paris; dpa picture alliance/ Alamy Stock Photo.

ization was necessary, one which took more seriously Heidegger's own emphasis on the "nihilating" force of nothingness (*das Nichts*) as a corollary of being. Once this force was properly taken into account and perhaps joined with the Nietzschean exodus beyond the "all-too-human" (or "last man"), it became imperative to insist more strongly than Heidegger had done on the rupture or disruption of ordinary human affairs or routinized states of being-in-the-world. As I understood him, it was precisely this rupture of the ordinary by the extraordinary or incommensurable that was at the heart of "deconstruction." I felt excited and thrilled by this rupture—but also disturbed and uneasy because it seemed to "disrupt" the primary accent of post-Husserlian phenomenology on concrete experience. While still quite inchoate at the time, this uneasiness would much later surface as a source of disagreement.[70]

Shortly thereafter I met with Michel Foucault. In his letter, he had asked me to see him at the Collège de France were he was teaching. The meeting time he had specified was right after a lecture he presented at the Collège. I was fascinated by his lecture, which dealt with a topic in the philosophy of language (and whose accent, in my understanding, signaled precisely the move from a structuralist to a poststructuralist type of explanation). I introduced myself to him afterward, but it turned out that he had an important engagement. Hence, he invited me to come the following afternoon to his apartment where we could talk undisturbed. Again, I was struck by the unassuming friendliness of this philosopher who, by that time, was already quite famous. The following afternoon was truly memorable. He lived in a comfortable suburban apartment, with all the walls lined to the ceiling with books. Like Derrida before him, he asked me about my background and my ongoing research. Our conversation soon came to the point. In some of his publications, he had written about a needed human "decentering" and, a bit provocatively, about the "end of man" or the "death of the subject."[71] My main question was how such phrases could be reconciled with any kind of phenomenology and also how they could leave room for human agency.

Foucault clearly was familiar with these questions—having been similarly pressed by both phenomenologists and critical theorists before. In a post-existentialist vein, he responded by pointing to the political and social struc-

Michel Foucault, Professor at the College de France in Paris; INTERFOTO/Alamy Stock Photo.

tures that severely constrained human initiatives—but added that these structures were not wholly determining and left space for human resistance and what he called "biopolitics" (inspired in part by Nietzsche). I was satisfied with his response—although I vaguely sensed the persistence in his argument of a dichotomy between structure and agency. (Much later, toward the end of his life, he proceeded to reformulate the issue in a less dichotomous way, by stressing the intrinsic agonal relation between human freedom and power without succumbing to critical or neo-Kantian moralism).[72] After about two hours of animated conversation, Foucault asked me whether I wanted to stay for supper. Not wishing to overstay my welcome, however, I declined—to my great later regret.

As was to be expected, my initial meetings with Derrida and Foucault in Paris had an aftermath: I maintained friendly relations with both until their deaths (Foucault in 1984 and Derrida in 2004). Although quibbling with them about some points, I continued to find their writings stirring and innovative. In this respect I found myself in disagreement with some other Continentalists like Taylor and Habermas. For Taylor, most French postmodernists were in danger of lapsing into the quagmire of subjectivism or relativism—a judgment which I found correct in some cases but wholly untenable in others. In turn, Habermas in his *Philosophical Discourse of Modernity* subjected both Derrida and Foucault to a scathing critique as heirs of Nietzsche (adding Adorno for good measure)—a judgment which I attributed to his excessive rationalist turn and hence could not accept.[73]

My main interest in Derrida, then and later, was for his early books, especially *Writing and Difference* and *Margins of Philosophy*. Later I became chagrined by a certain overindulgences in paradoxes and also an excessive celebration of rupture and radical transcendence, which seemed to me incompatible with the sobriety of phenomenology. What I found appealing in his later writings, however, was his critique of Eurocentrism (for example, in *The Other Heading*) and his eloquent plea in favor of cosmopolitanism and "cities of refuge" (in *Cosmopolites de tous les pays, encore un effort!*). I also was and continue to be inspired by his presentation of democracy as a "promise to come" (*a venir*).[74]

With a greater accent on power differentials, the critique of European or Western hegemony was also a central feature of Foucault's writings. Small wonder that this aspect provided strong support to a number of critical thinkers, including the literary critic Edward Said whom I also befriended during those years (and to whose magisterial work *Orientalism* I wrote a sequel titled *Beyond Orientalism*).[75] As noted by his opponents, Foucault was indeed an heir to Nietzsche—however with a twist. More clearly than the latter cared to state, power and "will to power" for Foucault were not so much dogmas or essential fixtures of reality but rather warning signals or reminders: signals that even the loftiest rhetoric and exalted ideals are often camouflages for the lust for power (and hence demand to be unmasked by a "hermeneutics of suspicion"). One of the most provocative warning signals was Foucault's comparison of modern society with Jeremy Bentham's idea of the *panopticon* (a structure permitting central surveillance). Once during a lecture given in the presence of American philosopher Richard Rorty, I referred approvingly to this comparison. During the question period Rorty challenged me (from the vantage of a comfortable American pragmatism), stating that there was no evidence for anything like a panopticon in Western societies. I was amazed. In retrospect I find that Foucault even understated the danger, given the ever-expanding security and surveillance state in our time. In this respect, Foucault's work will continue to present a clarion call for vigilance and for the preservation of human freedom in the face of governmental power and its totalitarian tendencies.[76]

The encounters with French intellectual life had whetted my appetite for more. During my year at Oxford I returned to Paris at least twice more. The first time I set aside for meetings with Gilles Deleuze and Jacques Lacan. This excursion did not go too well. Deleuze was teaching then in one of the satellite universities at the outskirts of Paris. Emboldened by my earlier good luck I had not written to him beforehand and simply went to his office. Maybe because of the lack of preliminaries, Deleuze proved to be not very approachable and preoccupied with other things. He did invite me, however, to one of his seminars—which proved to be disappointing. The room was filled to the brim with students, but their teacher arrived more than half an hour late and managed to irritate me with a number of odd mannerisms. (I am sure this was a very partial glimpse.) Lacan I never managed to see. His seminar was not publicized, with time and place only known to "insiders" (an aspect quite in keeping with the cryptic or hermetic character of his teachings). Fortunately, the next trip to Paris fully consoled me. Learning from mistakes, I had announced my visit to Claude Lefort who invited me to see him in the Institut de Sciences Politiques. Since he was a student and friend of the late Merleau-Ponty, his work was familiar and dear to me. A course he taught at the time—and to which he invited me—dealt with Machiavelli, and I was struck by the similarity of his treatment with the interpretation Merleau-Ponty had given earlier. Another teaching of Lefort that greatly impressed me was the notion of an "empty space" inhabiting modern democracy—an idea which I would later invoke in my own writings on democracy.[77]

Another, very pleasant encounter during this same trip was with Paul Ricoeur (to whom I had also announced myself). I had met him at several conferences before but had never made it a point to engage him in conversation. He was teaching at one of the satellite universities of the Sorbonne. After meeting him in his office, he took me for a walk on campus. Our conversation centered naturally on some topics he had written on and which preoccupied me: his relation to Gabriel Marcel and Karl Jaspers and, above all, his attempt to steer a course between Husserl and Heidegger. More recently, he had intervened in the Habermas-Gadamer debate and had placed himself in the middle—something that intrigued but did not entirely satisfy me. But he moved on from there to develop his own perspective on history, language, narrative, and other topics.[78] Generally speaking, I was struck—then as well as later—by the range and depth of his reflections. Later in his life, at the time of his retirement from the University of Chicago (where he had been teaching periodically), I had the occasion to present a kind of *laudatio* that centered on his "little ethics"—an ethics reconciling Aristotle and Kant—developed in *Oneself as Another*. After his death in 2005 I paid him a memorial tribute, relying on his lecture *Amour et Justice.* [79]

NOTRE DAME

Following my stay at Oxford, I took up my residence at Notre Dame where I had been hired the year before. My time in England had not quite yielded the result I had hoped for—at least in terms of the concern that had led me there: the question of language. During the ensuing months I continued to be troubled by the same question. I knew and was told from all sides that the twentieth century was marked by a "linguistic turn," a turn that placed language in the center of philosophical reflection. But what did this mean? What was the meaning of "language" to which philosophy presumably had turned?

My stay in England had familiarized me with empiricist, behavioral, and analytical conceptions of language. At the same time, my study of Continental philosophy, together with recent French postmodernism, had exposed me to transcendental, existential, structural, and poetic construals of language and the linguistic turn. As it appeared, contemporary thought finds itself immersed not only in a "Babel of tongues" but also in a Babel of conflicting conceptions and meanings of language. As it happens, just at this time I received an invitation from Loyola University in Chicago to present a week-long series of lectures on a topic of my choice. This invitation gave me the opportunity to sort out my thoughts about language and to place them in a coherent order or sequence. In preparing my lectures—which later were published under the title *Language and Politics*—I placed different approaches in an ascending sequence, moving from more objectivist construals (empiricism, behaviorism, structuralism) to more ontological or "disclosive" features of language (narrative, conversation, poetry).[80] I still feel somewhat at ease with this sequence.

Apart from the attempt to sort out my views on language, my first year at Notre Dame in many ways focused on Nietzsche. Partly in order to test the intellectual openness of the university, I had decided to teach my first graduate seminar there on Nietzsche—obviously a somewhat controversial figure at a Catholic school. Until barely fifteen years before my arrival, his works were still sequestered in a room of "prohibited books." To my surprise and joy, not only was I not reprimanded but I was actually encouraged and applauded by college administrators, including Father Hesburgh.[81] Apart from teaching my seminar, I had also invited Jacques Derrida as my first guest speaker at the university—and he chose as his topic "Nietzsche and Education."

Given Derrida's status as an international celebrity, and also given Notre Dame's genuine interest in education, his appearance on campus occasioned great excitement. I had secured the largest lecture hall on campus and, at the time of the lecture, the hall was filled to capacity, with people sitting in the chairs, in aisles and corridors. I had the pleasure of introducing Derrida to the audience, but unfortunately the lecture did not go as well as I had hoped. During the first hour, his talk was informative and exciting, with the audience sitting in rapt attention. The excitement, however, began to wear off during the second hour and, in the third hour, changed into a general restlessness. Given the crowded character of the hall, it was virtually impossible for people to leave. Sensing the mounting impatience, I gently reminded Derrida of the lateness of the hour—and he graciously stopped soon afterward. I discovered later that it was one of Derrida's habits to carry on at great lengths—not a very good habit, in my view, and also not fully in keeping with his emphasis on disruption.

Despite the awkwardness of the lecture, Derrida's visit was productive in another sense: it gave a strong boost to all the people—faculty and students alike—who were attracted to recent trends in Continental thought. After my arrival at Notre Dame, I soon became acquainted with a number of younger colleagues in different disciplines who, like me, were eager to explore innovative paths of intellectual inquiry. This group included a Continental philosopher (Stephen Watson), a sociologist versed in phenomenology and critical theory (Fabio Dasilva), and two members of the English department specializing in literary theory and hermeneutics (Joseph Buttigieg and Gerald Bruns). Together we designed a new course on the advanced undergraduate level that we called "Critical and Continental Thought." The idea of the course was to bring together different strands of recent European thought, from phenomenology and existentialism to Frankfurt School critical theory and deconstruction—as an antidote to mainstream forms of positivism and conceptual analysis. Team-taught by three or four members our group, the course was a success and attracted a sizeable number of students; as a result, we continued the practice for at least a decade.

On the whole, the period was one of the happiest for me as a teacher. Notre Dame attracted good and inquisitive students at both the undergraduate and graduate levels. There was a hopeful, forward-looking spirit at the university—and perhaps in the entire country (after the grim experiences of the

Vietnam War). On the undergraduate and graduate levels, the program in
political philosophy offered classes in the entire history of Western political
thought, dividing that history into four periods: with one colleague covering
Greek and Roman texts, another colleague medieval political ideas, a third
early modern thought, and the fourth (myself) covering late modern and
contemporary texts. In my graduate seminars I dealt with some of the luminaries of modern and contemporary European thought: from Hegel and
Nietzsche to Heidegger, Gadamer, Adorno, Habermas, Hannah Arendt, Merleau-Ponty, Derrida, and Foucault.

Apart from my teaching obligations, I continued to be active in various
professional organizations and associations. In the field of political science, I
regularly attended, and frequently presented papers at, the annual meetings of
the American Political Science Association. I also participated actively in a
section called Foundations of Political Theory, which, despite its heavy-
sounding title, catered mainly to the group of innovative and experimental
theorists I have mentioned before. Loosely structured and with very fluid
boundaries, the group included over the years such colleagues or friends like
William Connolly, Stephen White, George Kateb, Morton Schoolman, Iris
Marion Young, and Michael Shapiro (to mention just a few). Stephen White
was kind enough to put together the first edited volume on my writings;
Morton Schoolman encouraged me to write a book on Hegel for a series he
was editing; and Iris Marion Young became a close friend and interlocutor
(especially after her move to the University of Chicago). [82]

In the field of recent and contemporary philosophy, my intellectual
home—both then and later—was the Society for Phenomenology and Existential Philosophy (SPEP), whose annual meetings I faithfully attended. Invariably, these meetings would assemble learned experts on all the European
thinkers dearest to me and a host of others as well. Steady companions at
these meetings were my earlier colleagues at Purdue University, especially
Calvin Schrag and William McBride. Outside these gatherings I maintained
or established close ties with two philosophers with whom I edited books:
Thomas McCarthy and Seyla Benhabib. [83] Intermittently at some conferences
I also became acquainted with philosophers Richard Bernstein, David Rasmussen, and Judith Butler. Repeated visits to Germany gave me the opportunity to nurture a close bond with the German philosopher Bernhard Waldenfels whose Merleau-Pontyan leanings and emphasis on "border" crossings" I
fully shared. [84]

INDIA: BEYOND ORIENTALISM

In the midst of other professional activities, I received in 1984 an invitation
to participate in a conference on political theory in India. The conference was

to be held at the University of Baroda in the state of Gujarat whose vice chancellor then was the distinguished political thinker Bhikhu Parekh (now Lord Parekh). During those years, I was often invited to professional meetings of various kinds; hence, a conference in India seemed to be just a routine occurrence. As it turned out, however, this was far from being the case. In fact, the Baroda conference, and the experience of India associated with it, had a profound and lasting impact and became for me a kind of real *Kehre* or intellectual turning point.

Several factors accounted for this impact. One was the thoughtful and appealing structure of the conference. The meeting lasted for four days during which we were kept busy mostly with paper presentations and discussions. For the evenings, however, our hosts had prepared a variety of cultural and culinary treats. To start the evenings, the university and some other patrons offered sumptuous buffet dinners where we could savor the delicacies of Indian cuisine and especially the rich variety of vegetarian meals (which soon became my favorites). Following the dinners, cultural delights were in store. One evening was set aside for Indian folk dances with the dancers wearing colorful costumes from different parts of the country. Another evening was devoted to classical Indian music—whose sound was unfamiliar yet strangely enticing to me. Perhaps the high point of cultural events was an evening of classical Indian dance—again a completely new but deeply stirring experience for me. (I remember especially the powerful performance of a dancer impersonating Lord Shiva.)

Another, at least equally important factor contributing to the meeting's impact was the quality of the participants. The organizers had invited, next to me, several colleagues from America and England—some of whom were already quite well known. Thus, I became acquainted there with Kenneth Minogue (from the London School of Economics) and Richard Ashcraft, a leading Locke scholar.[85] The most interesting and impressive group of participants, however, was the large contingent of Indian colleagues. Apart from Bhikhu Parekh, whose writings on colonialism and Gandhi were familiar to me before, I had the good fortune of meeting a number of Indian theorists and intellectuals who then were unknown to me; limiting myself to a few, I want to mention V. R. Mehta (then at the University of Jaipur, but later vice chancellor at Delhi University); Ashis Nandy (from the Center for the Study of Developing Societies in Delhi); Partha Chatterjee (from the Center of Political Studies in Calcutta); and Thomas Pantham (a political theorist at the University of Baroda who became my closest friend in India).[86] There were also some slightly younger participants, like Rajeev Bhargava, Sudipta Kaviraj, and others.

What impressed me most about these Indian colleagues was their intellectual multilingualism or multiculturalism. As a rule they were thoroughly familiar with Western traditions of philosophy and political thought, while

Mohandas K. Gandhi, portrait, early 1940s.

also being steeped in the rich fabric of Indian culture. For me, this was a very unsettling state of affairs. The multilingualism of these colleagues made me painfully aware of my own Western parochialism. While they were able to discuss with me the thought of a Plato, Locke, or Nietzsche, I was unable to reciprocate, being woefully ignorant of Indian classical scriptures and of the great schools of Indian philosophy (like Nyaya or Vedanta). I decided then and there that this had to change and that I had to radically broaden my horizons beyond my Eurocentric confines. In a way, my decision was not haphazard or unprepared; it was supported by a number of earlier initiatives. Heidegger's post-Cartesian emphasis on openness to the "world," Gadamer's pursuit of hermeneutical dialogue, and postmodernism's insistence on self-decentering all conspired to favor an engagement with "otherness" over narrow self-enclosure. There is a difference, however, between cerebral awareness and practical conduct; in the case of French postmodernism, in particular, self-decentering often amounted to little more than engagement with a purely virtual or hypothetical otherness, to verbal flourishes eliding the difficult labor of practical learning.

Having become acquainted with numerous Indian colleagues during my first visit, I was invited subsequently to present lectures or seminars at many Indian universities or colleges. Thus, during the ensuing period, I traveled to India on an annual basis, speaking and interacting at a number of places, from Delhi and Jaipur to Bombay (now Mumbai), Pune, Calcutta, and Madras (now Chennai). Repeatedly I also visited Baroda to present lectures and be with my friend Pantham and his family. In Baroda, I also became acquainted with a professor of English literature, Prafulla Kar, who was organizing an interdisciplinary forum on contemporary theory, which I strongly supported and in which I would participate for several decades. It was during this time that I also developed a strong attachment to Gandhi and his legacy. Since Baroda is located in Gujarat, which was Gandhi's home state, I used my time there also to visit his birthplace (Porbander) and the places where he spent much of his time, especially Rajkot and Ahmedabad. In the latter city, I also visited his famous Satyagraha Ashram near the Sabarmati River.

Half a decade after my first visit to India, I successfully applied for a Fulbright research grant. Since many of my previous publications dealt with Frankfurt School thinkers, most of my colleagues expected me to go to Germany—and were surprised to learn that I had chosen India. My intent was really to immerse myself more deeply in Indian culture, philosophy, and literature, and a year-long stay (1991–1992) offered an ideal opportunity to do so. My chief residence during that stay was again Baroda where I felt more or less at home. During that year I devoted myself seriously to the study of Sanskrit, and I was lucky enough to engage the long-time head of the Sanskrit department, Professor Jani, as my tutor (during his occasional absences, his son agreed to guide me). As I discovered, despite many similarities with classical Greek, the Sanskrit grammar is even more complicated and differentiated, especially in terms of declensions and temporal modes. Due to the excellence of my tutors, I was eventually able—armed with a good dictionary—to tackle some of the classical Indian texts with a measure of confidence. At the same time, I tried to learn—but without formal instruction—the actual spoken language, which in that location is Gujarati (which is close to the more widely spoken Hindi). I strongly believe that, without some acquaintance or proficiency in the native language or languages, access to a foreign culture is extremely difficult (although perhaps not impossible). In my view, language—together with music, painting, and architecture—offers a privileged entry to a people's symbolic universe, to its imagination, its aspirations, triumphs and sorrows. Even when one cannot study a language thoroughly, one should listen to its sounds, its rhythmic cadences and intonations.

Intellectually, my main focus in that year was on Indian social and political thought during the preceding two centuries, that is, the time of the Indian "renaissance" and the struggle for independence.[87] In order to understand

that thought better, however, I also had to know more about the past, especially the great Indian philosophical traditions or "schools" (*darshanas*). As
good fortune would have it, I was invited several times to the old university
town of Poona or Pune, located in the center of India (the so-called Deccan).
Staying at the renowned De Nobile College, I became acquainted with several experts in that philosophical tradition, especially the great Shankara and
Vedanta scholar Fr. Richard De Smet, the Mimamsa scholar Fr. Francis
D'Sa, and the leading Nyaya expert Fr. John Vattanky.[88] Among them,
Father De Smet proved to be particularly friendly and hospitable. On several
occasions, he took me on sightseeing tours in the Deccan; once he also
accompanied me on a longer journey to Mysore with its royal palaces. In
Pune, I also met several times with Professor Sundara Rajan who taught
philosophy at the university there and was greatly interested in hermeneutics
and phenomenology (he passed away very prematurely a few years later). It
was also in Pune that I first met with the renowned German Indologist
Wilhelm Halbfass whose writings on the relations between India and the
West greatly impressed me.[89] During the same period, I immersed myself in
the rich reservoir of Indian religiosity: from Hinduism in its many forms to
Jainism, Buddhism, and Sufism. In this connection, I became attracted to the
great wealth of Indian *bhakti* (devotional) poetry, from Kabir and Mirabai to
Tukaram.[90]

Even after having spent a year in India, I felt that I had merely scratched
the surface. Above all, I had not sufficiently explored the rich local and
regional variety of Indian culture. Hence, I returned to the country repeatedly, although usually for shorter periods of time. One part I had not visited
was the north and northeast of the country, especially the ancient and holy
city of Banares (now Varanasi). One of the main attractions for me was the
old and prestigious Banares Hindu University. I was familiar with some
traditions of that university through the writing of a prominent Indian philosopher who had been trained there: J. L. Mehta. Starting his career in Banares,
Mehta later spent much time in Europe and America thoroughly absorbing
Western philosophical teachings but without ever renouncing his classical
Indian background—a blending which I found inspiring.[91] Some acquaintances invited me to present a series of lectures in Banares, and thus I came
to know some outstanding colleagues there. I also was able to experience the
truly vertiginal quality of that city with its narrow circular lanes and its
hallowed *ghats* leading to the Ganges River. From Banares it is only a short
distance to Sarnath and the famous "deer park" where the Buddha preached
his first sermon. Traveling still further north, I flew by plane to Kathmandu
in Nepal—a particularly enchanting place with its mixture of Hindu and
Buddhist culture and its proximity to the Himalayas. During ensuing years I
frequently visited Nepal and especially Kathmandu, never forgetting to pay

my respects to the temples of Pashupatinath, Boudhanath, and the "monkey temple" Swayambunath.

Another part of the country I was not really familiar with was the South. Some colleagues in Madras (Chennai) invited me to present some lectures at Madras University and also at Madras Christian College (where the philosopher and second Indian president Sarvepalli Radhakrishnan had studied). From that city I undertook several excursions or journeys. One was to the revered hilltop temple and pilgrimage site of Tirupati. Another, longer journey, undertaken by car with some colleagues, took me south along the famous "temple tour" including Kanchipuram, Mahabalipuram, Thiruvannamalai, Chidambaram, Tiruchi, and the huge temple city of Madurai. I finally ended up at the southern tip of India called Kanyakumari where I visited the celebrated Vivekananda shrine located on a rock island in the Indian Ocean.[92]

POLITICAL AND CONTINENTAL PHILOSOPHY

Alongside my repeated journeys abroad I carried on my regular teaching obligations at Notre Dame. As previously mentioned, we were fortunate during that period to attract good and highly motivated students which made teaching a pleasure, especially in graduate seminars. About a decade after joining Notre Dame, I was given a joint appointment in both philosophy and political science, a circumstance that allowed me to organize truly interdisciplinary courses. In my own research and writing, I felt a need to stake out my own path—however tentatively—in the midst of a welter of alternative perspectives and orientations. The initial result were two volumes titled respectively *Critical Encounters* (1987) and *Margins of Political Discourse* (1989). In the first book, I presented my critical readings (coupled with appreciation) of a large number of late-modern thinkers, from Nietzsche, Adorno, Habermas and Apel to Gadamer, Derrida, Ricoeur, Bernstein, Alasdair MacIntyre, and Michael Theunissen. Animated by a desire to understand others, these readings also helped me to understand myself better.[93] The second book was more political in orientation. It offered essays on Hegel's *Philosophy of Right*, Habermas's view of modernity, Bernhard Waldenfels's postmodernism (especially his book *Order at Twilight*), Ernesto Laclau's and Chantal Mouffe's analysis of the relation between democracy and hegemony, Ernst Bloch's *Principle of Hope*, and Wolfhart Pannenberg's *Anthropology in Theological Perspective* (the latter a prominent work in the emerging Continental perspective of political theology). The book also included my first essay on Mahatma Gandhi, whom I presented there as a "mediator between East and West."[94]

The most pressing intellectual issue for me during this time, however, was the need to sort out my competing allegiances to phenomenology and Heidegger, on the one hand, and Frankfurt School critical theory, on the other. The Habermas chapter in my *Margins* book was indicative of my evolving attitude. Focusing on his influential text *The Philosophical Discourse of Modernity,* written in 1985, I noticed Habermas's increasingly uncompromising turn to an abstract rationalism—what Merleau-Ponty would have called "intellectualism"—and his sidelining of practice and lived experience. I was chagrined by his dismissive treatment of Nietzsche and earlier Frankfurt theorists and his nearly dogmatic rejection of Heidegger's work. I also found unpersuasive and ungenerous the discussion of postmodern thinkers like Derrida and Foucault whose philosophical initiatives were rigidly subjected to the standards of a certain Enlightenment universalism.

In my estimate, the same rationalistic tendency was also evident in some of Habermas's other texts of this period, especially his writings on discourse ethics, universal pragmatics, and the communicative theory of action, where I discovered a strong emphasis on communicative rationality but little or no concern with action or praxis.[95] Both my intellectual discomfort and the effort to gain my own bearings are recorded in the book I published in 1991 under the title *Between Freiburg and Frankfurt: Toward a Critical Ontology* (the British edition was titled *Life-World, Modernity and Critique: Paths between Heidegger and the Frankfurt School*). As the title indicates, I tried to salvage some of the critical impulses of the Frankfurt School, while locating myself on the more ontological premises of Heidegger (and Adorno).[96]

Having wrestled with this issue and having found at least a tentative *modus vivendi,* I proceeded to move forward and to tackle two of the thinkers who, by that time, had acquired a predominant influence on me: Hegel and Heidegger. My friend Morton Schoolman—who then was editing a book series on modern political thought—invited me to contribute a volume, and after some soul-searching I settled on Hegel. The soul-searching was due mainly to my awareness of the formidable task involved in writing on the German idealist philosopher. Libraries have been written on nearly every facet of his work; moreover, his legacy is controversial and deeply contested. Some see him as the conservative defender of monarchy, while others praise him as a partisan of revolution; some celebrate his pervasive liberalism while others have denounced him as a devotee of the Prussian state (and even as a forebear of totalitarianism). By contrast to these assessments, what has always fascinated me in Hegel is his combination of ethical idealism with close attention to concrete life conditions (bypassing an abstract moralism). More specifically, I have valued and still value his defense of modern individual freedom (as a corrective to both the restrictive character of the ancient *polis* and the oppressiveness of modern absolutism) but also his effort to embed freedom in a web of ethical responsibilities, in what he called "ethical life"

(*Sittlichkeit*) ranging from the family to civil society and the state. In seeking to portray Hegel in this way, I received inspiration especially from the balanced and nonideological studies of Charles Taylor and Shlomo Avineri. The latter impressed me particularly with his sober discussion of Hegel's aloofness from the more virulent and populist forms of German Romanticism—an aloofness that, in my view, does not at all stand in the way of discovering in his late writings some democratic sympathies.[97]

An equally daunting task awaited me in my plans to write a book on Heidegger. Even more than Hegel's legacy, Heidegger's work is the target of virulent polemics. In an indiscriminate fashion, opponents denounce his entire opus as being hopelessly infected by the Nazi virus; seeking to bypass polemics, friends or supporters often portray this opus as entirely nonpolitical, as an exemplar of pure or perennial philosophy. The more I was working myself into Heidegger's writings, the less plausible these alternatives appeared to me. The condemnation of his foes seemed to me lopsided and untenable given the nonideological character of *Being and Time* and the other writings; on the other hand, the claim of "pure" philosophy seemed implausible in the case of a thinker who defined human *Dasein* as "being-in-the-world" (where "world" necessarily includes the social world). Hence, I was trying to find another avenue for reading Heidegger, an avenue bypassing these sterile controversies; the result was *The Other Heidegger* (1993).

The aim of that text was to uncover possibly fruitful contributions of Heidegger's work to contemporary social and political thought, contributions that might shed some light on dilemmas arising from the postmodern critique or demise of Cartesianism. Proceeding along this road, I concentrated mainly on four topical areas: the status of the "subject" as a political agent; the character of political community (construed in postmetaphysical terms); the issue of cultural and political development (or modernization); and finally the problem of an emerging cosmopolis or world order beyond the confines of the Westphalian system of nation-states. The book also dealt with numerous other issues, including Heidegger's relation to democracy, his conception of ethics and justice, and his notion (heavily indebted to Hölderlin) of a "homecoming through otherness." In writing the book, my conviction steadily grew that Heidegger's work is not only free of fascist overtones but points in a direction wholly at odds with fascist and other totalitarian agendas.[98]

The years leading up to the publication of *The Other Heidegger* were full of other travel opportunities that helped inform my scholarship. In the mid-1980s I had been invited once again to serve as visiting professor at the University of Hamburg. During that time I made it a point to renew my acquaintance or friendship with Bernhard Waldenfels who then was teaching at the University of Bochum (although he maintained his regular home in Munich). To my knowledge, he was really the only well-known German professor who displayed a genuine interest in, and understanding of, recent

French philosophy (from Merleau-Ponty to Derrida and Emmanuel Levinas). Like me, he was disenchanted with Habermasian rationalism and found relief in the subtlety of postmodern French thought. In the spring semester of 1988, I served as the Werner Marx Visiting Professor in Philosophy at the New School for Social Research in New York—a position held during the preceding year by Waldenfels.[99]

I felt deeply honored by that appointment, remembering the long line of famous German émigrés who had taught at that institution (from Aron Gurwich and Alfred Schutz to Leo Strauss and Hannah Arendt). At the time of my visit, several new faculty members had just joined the department, among them Richard Bernstein and Agnes Heller (the former student of Georg Lukács). Both intellectually and personally, their presence at the institution proved immensely rewarding. Although attracted to Habermasan critical theory Bernstein, in my view, carried on the best tradition of Deweyan pragmatism (something I found missing in Richard Rorty, for example).[100] On the other hand, moving forward from humanist Marxism, Heller had developed a unique blend of liberal-social existentialism with which I could find points of contact. Another colleague I came to know and appreciate at the New School was Reiner Schürmann, one of the finest Heidegger scholars it has been my pleasure to meet. His treatment of such Heideggerian notions as "difference" and "praxis" is still unparalleled today (he sadly passed away not long after my visit).[101]

MULTICULTURALISM AND GLOBALIZATION

Viewed on the surface, my stay at the New School as well as my writings on Hegel and Heidegger might seem as a relapse into the kind of intellectual Eurocentrism from which I was trying to extricate myself. This view, however, neglects the complexity of the "hermeneutical circle." As hermeneutical philosophy (Gadamer in particular) teaches, moving out into unfamiliar terrain—the unfamiliarity of texts, cultures, or traditions—does not really involve the complete abandonment or discarding of one's own background and familiar frames of significance. On the contrary, it is precisely these frames that allow one to approach alien meanings or life-forms in a questioning and hence undogmatic mode conducive to a possible learning experience. By the same token, pursued in a genuinely dialogical mode, such questioning is liable to call one's own perspective into question, triggering a modification or correction of initial assumptions. Thus, the best of Europe's philosophical traditions (in my view) points beyond Eurocentric self-enclosure—and this is true of the legacy of Hegel as well as that of Heidegger (and his followers). Despite certain subjectivist and world-historical biases, Hegel's emphasis on the need for mutual "recognition" transgresses any arrogant unilateralism. In the same manner, Heidegger's entire philosophy can be (and should be) seen as a rebellion against anthropocentrism and against any form of cognitive self-sufficiency associated with (aspects of) the European Enlightenment. Hence, my studies of Hegel and Heidegger were not meant to anchor me more securely in Western thought but to serve as possible springboards to broader, cross-cultural or transcultural explorations.

As it happened, the time seemed eminently propitious for such an undertaking. With the collapse of the Soviet Union in 1989, the Cold War came officially to an end, and with it a period during which humanity had been divided into two ideologically frozen blocs. As it seemed to me—looking at it from a Socratic angle—the Cold War had weighed like an incubus on humankind, forcing it to opt between two dead-end roads: a faceless collectivism and an atomistic individualism. As can readily be seen, both options were derivatives of a certain abstract Enlightenment agenda: on the one hand, the universalism of calculating egos; on the other hand, the generality of a (presumably universal) "class." With the lifting of this incubus, new possibilities of human and social life came into view, possibilities that encouraged and required creative social imagination. Foremost among these possibilities were new combinations or interpenetrations of universality and particularism, of identity and difference, of enlightened modernist and recalcitrant postmodern vistas. It was in this arena of complex combinations and contestations that the emerging fields of multicultural and intercultural studies found their inspiration and legitimating resources.

In my own case, the end of the Cold War gave a welcome boost to the investigation of non-Western cultures that I had begun in 1984. Following my Fulbright year in India, annual visits had further cemented my bond with that country, while also deepening my awareness and appreciation of India's ethnic, religious, and cultural diversity. As I came to realize, it was Gandhi's genius to lead the country to independence not by promoting a bland conformity but by seeking to reconcile antagonistic strands in a (more or less) harmonious fabric of differences. In this respect, Gandhi seemed to be a follower more of Montesquieu and Herder than of Rousseau and the Jacobins. In contemporary India, I found the Gandhian spirit still alive in many places, but especially at the Centre for the Study of Developing Societies (CSDS) in Delhi—a place I visited repeatedly over the years and whose senior members (especially Rajni Kothari and Ashis Nandy) became good friends.

As I should add, however, India for me was not a final resting place. As Europe before, India came to serve as a launching pad for further explorations. Intrigued or enticed by the Buddhist legacies in India, I followed the historical lines of Buddhist migration from India—first along the southern (or Theravada) route leading to Burma and Thailand; and secondly along the northern (or Mahayana) route leading from Nepal and Tibet to China and

Japan. In East Asia, as we know, Buddhism encountered venerable indigenous traditions with which it would compete and intermingle, especially
Confucianism and Daoism. In India another important cultural and religious
strand that fascinated me was the long legacy of Islam, which, looking back
in time, stretches from the Mughal empire to the beginning of the Delhi
sultanate almost a thousand years ago.

As it happened, during the 1990s, I was invited to present lectures in
several Muslim countries. Thus, early in that decade, I was asked to give
talks in Egypt at the University of Cairo where the philosopher and Ricoeur
student Hassan Hanafi was teaching. Our shared attachment to hermeneutics
quickly established a friendly bond between us. In Cairo, I also became
acquainted with the great scholar of Islamic thought Father Georges Anawati
who kindly gave me a scholarly tour through the marvelous library at his
Institut Dominicaín d'Etudes Orientales. A few years later I was invited to
Morocco, more specifically to the University of Rabat, where I had the great
pleasure of meeting and conversing with the neo-Averroist philosopher Muhammad al-Jabri, a conversation that was subsequently continued and deepened. During the same decade, I also participated in several conferences in
Istanbul, Turkey. The first conference—a kind of traveling symposium—led
us from Istanbul all the way toward the eastern city of Dyarbakir near the
Iraqi frontier. It was at that time that I first made the acquaintance of the
Iranian philosopher Abdulkarim Soroush and of the Turkish professor Ahmet
Davutoglu (who several years later become Turkish minister of foreign affairs and finally prime minister). At the time of Davutoglo's shift to public
office, I in a way inherited some of his former students; two of them came to
the United States where I served as their doctoral advisor. To round out this
part of my narrative I might add that, quite a few years later, I had the
occasion to write a memorial tribute for al-Jabri and also for Hanafi's former
student Nasr Abu Zayd (both passed away in 2010).[102]

Cross-cultural inquiry for me involved travels but also scholarly work. As
it happens, the discipline of philosophy in the West includes a relatively
well-developed subfield called comparative philosophy. I soon became a
devoted participant in that field. Some of the work in that area is supported
and carried on by academic centers and institutes, as well as by a variety of
professional associations. Probably the most well-known and prestigious institute of comparative philosophy is the so-called East-West Center at the
University of Hawaii; loosely affiliated with it is the Society for Asian and
Comparative Philosophy (SACP). To my great delight, I was invited to participate in some of the major international conferences organized by the East-
West Center—occasions that allowed me to befriend some of the founders of
cross-cultural philosophical studies like Eliot Deutsch, Gerald Larson, Raimon Panikkar, Tu Weiming, Roger Ames, Henry Rosemont Jr., and Marietta
Stepaniants.[103] I soon became also a regular member of the Society for Asian

and Comparative Philosophy, whose annual meetings (held at the quiet retreat of Asilomar at the Pacific coast) greatly facilitated my access to Asian
thought. For many years, my participation in that society paralleled my participation in the Society for Phenomenology and Existential Philosophy; both
societies were for me invaluable training grounds: in the one case (SPEP)
deepening my familiarity with Continental philosophy; in the other case
(SACP) strengthening my acquaintance with East Asian and South Asian
traditions of thought. Like the former, the latter society also gave me the gift
of a rich reservoir of new friends and colleagues. Among them I want to
single out—apart from the founders mentioned above—the renowned Gandhi scholar Douglas Allen and the Panikkar students Joseph Prabhu and
Michiko Yusa.[104] At a later point, during 2004–2005, I served as president of
SACP.

In connection with my participation in the East-West Center and SACP, I
should also mention a discovery that deeply influenced me: the discovery of
Japanese Buddhism in the form of the Kyoto School. The discovery was
unplanned and nearly accidental. On the recommendation of a colleague, I
picked up a book by the Kyoto philosopher Keiji Nishitani titled (in English
translation) *Religion and Nothingness*.[105] The book blew me away. I had
never read anything about religion couched in this language. I was familiar,
through other readings, with the centrality of the notion of emptiness (*sunyata*) in Buddhist thought. But Nishitani stood out by the depth of his insights
and the breadth of his discussion. In addition to being an eminent Buddhist
thinker, he was also an erudite comparative philosopher. Thus he was able to
compare the Buddhist notion of emptiness with important strands in modern
Western philosophy, especially existentialism and Heideggerian ontology.
Prompted by his work, I ventured myself into this comparative arena by
juxtaposing Japanese Mahayana teachings and Heidegger's notion of nothingness (*das Nichts*).[106]

Through the study of Nishitani, I became familiar with other members of
the Kyoto School, especially his great teacher Kitaro Nishida and his fellow
students Haime Tanabe and Masao Abe. As it happens, my Japanese friend
Michiko Yusa at that time was composing a major intellectual biography on
Nishida.[107] Several visits to Kyoto and its numerous Zen temples soon made
that city another home away from home, and I was able to travel to Osaka,
Sendai, Okinawa, and the Peace Park in Hiroshima as well.

In the course of these years I observed that the comparative subfield in
philosophy was not shared by political theory, which still tended to be a
strictly Western or Eurocentric enterprise closely tied to the canon, from
Plato to Hegel and Nietzsche. It became one of my main endeavors during
this period to inaugurate or launch what I called comparative political theory
in a global or cross-cultural perspective. In 1997, a leading journal of political thought invited me to put together an entire issue devoted to this emerg-

ing field. In revised form, the issue became the lead volume in a book series launched by Lexington Books in 1999 under the title *Global Encounters: Studies in Comparative Political Theory*.[108] (Lexington Books then was in the competent hands of its director Stephen Wrinn who subsequently moved to the University of Kentucky Press and more recently to University of Notre Dame Press). I need to add that my efforts in comparative political theory were greatly supported and strengthened by the work of several colleagues and friends, especially Bhikhu Parekh, Anthony Parel, Hwa Yol Jung, Charles Butterworth, and to some extent Charles Taylor—as I pointed out in a key essay introducing the new field to the political science profession.[109]

DARK CLOUDS: WARS AGAIN

The approach of the new millennium gave rise to widespread apprehensions and a host of diverse prognoses. In the eyes of some, the millennium was bound to be ushered in by large-scale catastrophes and conflagrations. For others, the new era carried with it the promise of vastly improved conditions in the world. A major proponent of the latter view was Mohammad Khatami, then president of the Republic of Iran. Sensing a wave of goodwill in many countries following the end of the Cold War, Khatami announced the dawn of a genuine "dialogue among civilizations" replacing the older model of warfare—an idea that enjoyed broad resonance and also appealed to me. Endorsing the initiative and seeking to bolster international good will, the United Nations—through a resolution of its General Assembly—proceeded to proclaim 2001 as the Year of Dialogue Among Civilizations.

Unfortunately, the global climate changed dramatically in that same year: The hopes for global peace through dialogue were dashed or at least severely dimmed later in 2001 by the attack on the New York Trade Center on September 11. With this attack, the old Westphalian system of interstate conflict was to all intents and purposes reinstated, albeit with a novel twist. In lieu of its traditional focus on the actions of nation-states, warfare was now in a way generalized or globalized, making room for the role by violent nonstate actors. With this change, the potential for global violence was vastly increased, with the result that whole populations were placed under the harsh regime of fear or terror. It was due to this latter result that leading politicians soon labeled (or perhaps mislabeled) the new scenario as the era of "terror wars," with the whole world serving as a global battlefield.

In Western societies, September 11 triggered an almost instant hardening of lines and a return to the primacy of national interests. In America, in particular, the old Cold War mentality powerfully reasserted itself with its vision of a radically polarized world, now pitting the West mainly against Islam or Islamic countries. As in former times, political antagonism was soon intensified by resort to moralistic and quasi-religious rhetoric. While previously the Soviet Union had been labeled an "evil empire," now the Islamic world, or at least some Muslim countries, were denounced as part of a threatening "axis of evil." The mobilization of incendiary rhetoric soon produced its predictable result: first, the war against the Taliban in Afghanistan, and second, in the offensive attack on Iraq. Whereas, in the former case, some connection with September 11 could loosely be established, the second case bypassed cause-and-effect considerations and proceeded mainly on a visceral level, aided and abetted by media manipulation and ominous references to weapons of mass destruction. Once war was unleashed, of course, social and political life was steadily subordinated to national security interests, which frequently took the shape of new nationalistic and xenophobic legislation. In lieu of good will and dialogue, international politics came to be subjected again to the harsh dictates of the "friend-enemy" formula—with the customary result of mental regimentation.

There was another carry-over from the earlier Cold War era: the glorification of capitalist free enterprise. There was a rapid expansion of military arsenals alongside socioeconomic "downsizing" and privatization. Curiously (and incoherently) the glorification of private profit-seeking was accompanied by the upsurge of Christian fundamentalism (the latter perhaps a mirror-reflex of the perceived upsurge of religion elsewhere). The ideology of neo-conservatism—an amalgam of disparate elements (only linked by a shared elitist agenda): capitalist neoliberalism, social and religious conservativism, and militaristic expansionism—experienced a potent resurgence.

These developments cast deep shadows on the world and inflicted untold sufferings on many people. For me, these years were a time of nightmares, bringing back memories of my childhood—when wars had been unleashed wantonly and when elementary standards of civility had been flagrantly brushed aside. I was aghast by the disregard for rudimentary principles of international law, especially by the dismissal of the Geneva Conventions and the sometimes flagrant espousal of torture practices. My dismay was deepened by another memory of my youth: the widespread silence, amounting to complicity, of academic intellectuals in the face of blatant political and military abuses. As in the case of totalitarian regimes, civic courage is in short supply when livelihoods and academic careers are deemed to be in peril. As it became clear, so-called liberal regimes in the West—heirs to a long tradition of civil liberties—are not shielded from the sway of oppressive conformism and mind control. As in the case of the earlier Cold War, ideological polarization after September 11 tended to engender widespread intellectual timidity: instead of exploring new vistas or horizons, many intellectuals became again backward-looking and fond of rehearsing time-honored "verities" or founding narratives (unless they directly allowed themselves to be ideologically coopted).

Being located in a private Catholic university, I was shielded from the worst effects of the discussed polarization—or at least so it appeared at the beginning. Notre Dame boasts a long tradition of the humanities that cannot quickly be overturned. Moreover, there was the strong impact of Father Hesburgh's progressive legacy. Yet things began to change, subtly but steadily. Hesburgh had retired in 1987, after thirty-five years of service. His successors were well-intentioned people but overshadowed by a new breed of academic leaders dedicated mostly to "administering" the university rather than providing intellectual guidance or inspiration. Their influence was powerfully supported by a major trend sweeping through Western universities and colleges: the corporatization of academic life, meaning the (tendential) transformation of academic institutions into forms of corporate business. As a result of this trend, many American universities were placed into the hands of managers often equipped with good business training but with little or no training in the humanities and little or no aptitude for communicating with faculty in the liberal arts. Although more slow in coming than elsewhere, corporatism took a toll at Notre Dame as well (as illustrated by the fact that one of the last humanistic economics departments in the country was abolished in favor of one focused on econometrics). What gave to corporatism at Notre Dame a special twist was the rise of conservative tendencies in the Church, in the sense that the reformist legacy of Vatican II (supported by Hesburgh) was tendentially muffled in favor of clerical hierarchy and authority.[110]

Unfortunately, the sketched trends also impinged on my own field of teaching where political theorizing was more than ever limited to the rehearsal of canonical texts. Given the inhospitable environment, I found it preferable and more rewarding to concentrate more and more on my own work. The titles of my books written during this period clearly testify to my commitment to an "other thinking" or to alternative political and intellectual scenarios. Just before the turn of the century I published *Alternative Visions: Paths in the Global Village* (1998). The paths delineated in the book were meant to be alternative road markers pointing beyond both an abstract universalism and an ethnocentric particularism and, above all, beyond the pursuit of unilateral imperial hegemony. Among the thinkers I invoked as guides were Johann Gottfried Herder, Gandhi, Amilcar Cabral, and a number of contemporary Indian thinkers—especially Kothari and Nandy—concerned with forms of social development different from the Western model.[111] Another Asian thinker who began to loom large on my intellectual horizon was the Malaysian Muslim Chandra Muzaffar whose writings relentlessly champion the cause of justice in the face of injustices and corruption anywhere in the world.[112]

At the beginning of the new millennium *Alternative Visions* was followed by a text whose title even more clearly pinpointed its perspective: *Achieving*

Our World: Toward a Global and Plural Democracy (2001). Taking its bearings again from Herder and his heirs, the text championed an approach designed to reconcile global interactions with respect for cultural pluralism and diversity; in the language of Richard Falk—with whom I interacted increasingly during this time (and who soon became a friend)—the approach favored a popular "globalization from below," that is, one anchored in local or indigenous aspirations, over a hegemonic "globalization from above." In addition to exploring the local-global nexus, the text also examined forms of "self-other" relations (as a backdrop to cross-culturalism) drawing on philosophical insights culled from Schrag, Waldenfels, Derrida, and Ricoeur.[113] The most sustained effort to counter the resurgent Cold War syndrome, however, was my book *Dialogue Among Civilizations: Some Exemplary Voices* (2002)—a text which, relying on hermeneutical premises, highlighted such diverse figures as the Muslim philosopher Ibn Rushd (Averroes), the German poet Goethe, the Spanish-Indian thinker Raimon Panikkar, the Iranian philosopher Abdulkarim Soroush, and (again) Gandhi.[114]

Contrary to initial predictions, the Iraq War—unleashed in 2003—proved to be protracted and seemingly unmanageable. Daily media reports recounted the enormous costs of the war in terms of infrastructure and loss of lives (with estimates ranging between 100,000 and 500,000 civilian lives). The experience of the early war years greatly aggravated me and intensified my commitment to alternative agendas. The most important alternative agenda for me was peace. On a personal level, the intensity of that commitment can be gauged from my book *Peace Talks—Who Will Listen?* (2004). Recalling the important mentor of my youth, the book paid tribute to the great peace-loving sage of Rotterdam: Erasmus. The title of the book itself was culled from one of Erasmus' own texts, *The Complaint of Peace* (*Querela pacis*) where he allows peace to address us in her own voice but wonders "who will listen?" Apart from guiding readers through some of Erasmus' memorable writings, *Peace Talks* also explored the longstanding efforts of "civilizing humanity" (through a global "law of peoples"), Hannah Arendt's still pertinent reflections on violence, and Gandhi's lifelong embrace of nonviolence (with specific reference to the prospect of nonviolent relations between Hindus and Muslims in India).[115]

A companion piece of that text was a book published shortly afterward titled *Small Wonder: Global Power and Its Discontents* (2005). In one sense, the phrase "small wonder" was meant as an antidote to the modern cult or idolatry of bigness: big power, big wealth, big technology, big bigness. In another sense, the phrase pointed to the recessed or inconspicuous manner in which anything like wonder or enchantment can survive in our massively saturated world. Hints or clues of this second meaning can be found in Indian novelist Arendhati Roy's *The God of Small Things*, Walter Benjamin's "Angelus Novus," Gianni Vattimo's *pensiero debole*, and Heidegger's recessed "sheltering" of the divine.[116]

IN SEARCH OF THE GOOD LIFE

The same period, the early years of the new millennium, saw me busy in many other ways. On a regular basis, as a senior Fellow, I participated in the conferences and programs of the Kroc Institute for International Peace Studies at Notre Dame. Periodically I was also involved in meetings organized by UNESCO in Paris and other parts of the world. Apart from attending gatherings of philosophical societies, my concern with the state of international politics prompted me to frequent the annual meetings of the International Studies Association (ISA), whose Global Development Section in 2003 honored me with a Distinguished Scholar Award. Feeling increasingly the weight of my years, I retired from the university in 2005 as a full-time faculty member, having completed forty-five years as a college teacher. Notre Dame was gracious enough to offer me a staggered retirement, allowing me to reduce my obligations steadily over the ensuing five years. Apart from the dismal political situation, an important factor prompting me to seek retirement was the experience with a kind of cancer that entailed a drawn-out series of treatments and procedures. Another factor was the realization of the progressive thinning out of the ranks of close acquaintances and age cohorts: Gadamer passed away in 2002, Bobbio in 2004, Derrida in the same year, Ricoeur in 2005, and Rorty in 2007, followed soon by my Indian philosopher friend Daya Krishna.[117]

The cited experiences, and especially the departure of close friends, brought home to me the reality of my own finitude, the fact—previously repressed or brushed aside—that I had only a limited number of years to live. At this point, the question arose for me how to spend the remaining years most sensibly or most fruitfully and, more particularly, how I could channel my scholarly endeavors toward genuinely meaningful things—and away from issues of a merely fashionable or trendy character. Reflecting on this matter, it became clear to me that the central issue—the issue more important than all others—is how to live one's life and how to live properly and peacefully with other human beings in a community. As it happened, my wife and I at one time were making a tour of Italy where we also stopped in Siena. The town hall of that city contains a series of beautiful and pertinent frescoes that depict "The Allegory of Bad Government," "The Effects of Bad Government in Town and Country," "The Allegory of Good Government," and "The Effects of Good Government in Town and Country." The allegorical depiction of bad government portrays in vivid scenes rulers obsessed with power, lust, and greed; the consequences are shown to be strife, violence, mayhem, and general devastation. The allegorical image of good government depicts rulers dedicated to justice and the observance of cardinal virtues; the effects of this regime are happiness and flourishing of people in city and country. In line with these good effects, the room is appropriately also called Peace Hall.

Studying and reflecting on these allegorical pictures I remembered a teaching that, as an undercurrent, had accompanied me all my life but that I had not sufficiently brought into focus: the teaching that the goal of public existence is the cultivation of an ethically "good life." The teaching goes back to the Greeks, especially Aristotle; but in modern times it has tended to be sidelined by the stress on self-interest, individual rights, and private happiness—with dubious results. Despite undeniable advances in freedom and material well-being, modern times are also replete with all the ills of bad government: warfare, genocide, and ethnic cleansing, with the specter of nuclear holocaust never far in the distance. Pondering the situation, the issue of the "good life" appeared to me as a proper theme for one's twilight years. Yet caution also seemed indicated. Not being a fundamentalist (nor an anti-modernist), it was clear to me that the good life could not simply be invoked as a *deus ex machina* nor be foisted on people from on high. In an age of democracy, the good or bad effects of government cannot simply be ascribed to public officials or elites but have to be traced to the dispositions of ordinary people (seen as rulers in a democracy). Moreover, given the cultural, ethnic, and religious diversity of modern democracies, the meaning of the good life is bound to be subject to multiple construals or interpretations. Any attempt to impose one single conception is bound to be seen as antidemocratic and a dangerous step toward totalitarianism. What came to my rescue in this context was an insight gleaned from personal experience: the fact that one can cherish and even love a person without fully knowing or being able to define that person in every way. Religiously, it is acknowledged that one can love God or the divine without epistemic cognition or comprehension. A similar insight seems applicable to the good life.[118]

Another factor supporting my endeavor was the upsurge of the concept of "virtue ethics" in recent times—an upsurge due in no small measure to my Notre Dame colleague Alasdair MacIntyre. In the opening section of his *After Virtue*, MacIntyre had presented a devastating scenario where, due to some massive catastrophe, all the traces or memories of traditional virtue had been erased, leaving behind people in a Hobbesian state of nature.[119] In my own estimate, the portrayal was not far from reality in many Western societies. The concept of "virtue ethics" was congenial to me and preferable to most competing moral or ethical theories. Among these alternatives, utilitarianism had never much appealed to me due to its stress on external consequences and the quantitative summation of preferences; nor had hedonism been attractive (in its simplistic form). The case was somewhat different with "deontology" or the stress on ethical "duty"—and this mainly due to my longstanding respect and admiration for Kant's moral theory (a respect that did not always carry over to neo-Kantian epigones). In our time marked by consumerism and private self-satisfaction, Kant's prioritizing of duty seemed indeed desirable as a corrective. What left me frustrated, however, was Kant's division between inner and outer domains and the insufficient attention given (in my view) to the cultivation of dispositions needed for the performance of duties.

With its borrowing from Aristotelian teachings, virtue ethics provided precisely the antidote to the latter defects. Nevertheless, my endorsement was limited by two considerations. First of all, as practiced by professional philosophers, virtue ethics has confined itself mainly to private conduct while leaving aside the public or political domain. Second, as a corollary of this limitation, practitioners tended to pay insufficient attention to democratic pluralism and the importance of modern freedom in the pursuit of competing ends.[120] Attentive to these considerations, my book *In Search of the Good Life* (2007) did not present a full-fledged theory or doctrine of the good life but rather portrayed the latter as a pathway or search, in fact, as an infinite horizon stimulating human aspirations in different forms and from different angles. In lieu of a theory, the first part of the book offers a series of stories or narratives illustrating how the good can be, and has been, searched for in exemplary ways. To cast the net widely, examples are taken from both Western and non-Western cultures and from different time periods. Thus, in the context of the Middle Ages, two exemplary voices are taken from the West (St. Bonaventure and Nikolaus of Cusa) and one from the East (the Indian poet-saint Jñanadev). In the modern period, narratives deal with Leibniz's encounter with the "natural theology" of the Chinese, Montesquieu's reflections on Islam (in his "Persian Letters,") and Friedrich Schiller's sketch for an "aesthetic education" of humankind.

Turning to the recent and contemporary period, the text ponders how searching for the good life can serve as an inspiration for pedagogy in our troubled times. Among the issues discussed are the role of the classics (Eastern and Western) in contemporary education; proper and improper ways of spreading democracy globally (through military force or good example); the problem of politicized evil (surfacing in slogans like the "axis of evil"); the possibility of multiple and transnational citizenship (as an antidote to chauvinism); and the proper role of religion in our predominantly secular culture. As it seems to me, civic pedagogy in all these cases means a move away from private selfishness and self-enclosure in the direction of the cultivation of cross-cultural dispositions or virtues.[121]

DEMOCRACY AND RETURN TO NATURE

The book was published when, politically and ethically, the affairs of the world were still hanging in the balance. In 2008, however, elections in America brought a change that—in the perception of many people—signaled a turn from military unilateralism in the direction of greater intercultural comity and respect. The change promised to lift political life—which had sunk into the quagmire of cynicism and corruption for more than a decade—onto a new level, thereby restoring to it some of the luster attributed to it by the ancients. Given the prestige enjoyed by democratic politics around the world, was it perhaps possible to lift democracy also to a new level of ethical responsibility, beyond its prevalent association with individual and collective self-interest? This question greatly intrigued me and quickly became a dominant intellectual passion, setting me on the road of a new scholarly endeavor that subsequently I would call "the promise of democracy."

The central issue fascinating me was that of popular rule, or rather the confluence of rule and non-rule. How is it possible for people to rule democratically, that is, without coercively ruling over others? This, I realized, can only happen through ethical self-rule—which the Mahatma Gandhi had called *swaraj*. Here again ancient teachings are relevant and intersect with modern and contemporary experiences. As may be recalled, classical thought distinguished between good and bad political regimes, with the difference residing in the objective of rule: while bad regimes promote the self-interest of rulers (kings or princes), the objective of good rulership is justice and the well-being of all the people. In large measure, this teaching has been forgotten in modern democracies, partly due to their origin. Arising out of a rebellion against traditional regimes, the gist of democracy is often found in popular self-assertion, that is, in the people's exercise of unlimited power or sovereignty. However, can people not also govern unjustly, selfishly, and oppressively? Hence, the classical distinction resurfaces. Seen from this angle, democracy as popular rule means a regime in which people can rule themselves noncoercively and justly, with an eye toward the common good.

Fortunately, in studying the history of democracy, I discovered an alternative genealogy that emphasizes precisely this aspect—a genealogy leading from Aristotle and Cicero to Montesquieu and Alexis de Tocqueville. Although not himself a democratic thinker, Hegel's stress on the primacy of "ethical life" also provides inspiration along similar lines. However, the most powerful contribution to an ethical conception of democracy in late modernity was made by John Dewey—a thinker whom I had largely bypassed in earlier years but who now became for me a rich source of political reflection. This turn to Deweyan pragmatism, in turn, brought to the forefront an issue not commonly considered in democratic theory: the issue of the meaning of action or practical agency. As it dawned on me, to avoid coercion or manipu-

lation, democratic action cannot be equated with willful or selfish intervention but has to take the form of interactive generosity. At this point, Martin
Heidegger's notion of "letting be" came to my assistance, especially his idea
of a "primordial praxis" allowing a general flourishing of social life. This
idea, it seems to me, can without great difficulty be connected with classical
paideia and the cultivation of generously defined republican virtues—a legacy largely sidelined in recent intellectual developments in favor of "will to
power" and "friend-enemy" formulas. My book *The Promise of Democracy*
(2010), in any event, was meant to provide an antidote both to the equation of
democracy with selfishness and to the looming scenario of unlimited "terror
wars"—thus honoring the Deweyan as well as the Gandhian spirit. [122]

As I realize, the notion of an ethical democracy inspired by public virtues
runs into a major roadblock today: the widespread hesitation to employ "virtue" language in the public domain (whatever its significance in private life
may be). Although it may have been privileged in ancient times—one often
hears—virtue has now lost its appeal and been replaced by the ideas of
freedom, liberty, and liberation. Far from being a merely academic issue, the
antinomy in late modernity has acquired a political cast, surfacing in the
mode of "culture wars." In these wars, virtue typically assumes a mainly
restorative or backward-looking quality, becoming associated with the preservation of the past including traditional structures of (political and religious)
authority. On the other hand, freedom tends to be equated with individualism, social randomness, fragmentation, and (perhaps) lawlessness. Perhaps
due to my old Erasmian leanings, culture wars never held much attraction for
me. Sensing the importance of the issue, however, I decided to make it the
focus of another study, which subsequently came to be called *Integral Pluralism: Beyond Culture Wars* (2010). [123] In lieu of associating virtue with
traditional uniformity (or "monism") and modern freedom with random pluralization, I found it advisable to reformulate the issue in a triadic way: by
distinguishing between traditional unity, modernist "dualism" or bifurcation,
and "integral" pluralism or holistic differentiation. [124]

While pursuing my academic work I continued to learn by traveling and
attending international conferences. Thus, I took part in the UNESCO-spon-
sored World Days of Philosophy in Rabat, Morocco, in 2007 and in Moscow
in 2009. In 2008, I was asked to serve as a plenary speaker at the World
Congress of Philosophy held in Seoul, Korea—a visit that became the
launching pad for a number of later visits to that city. During the same
period, I also worked on a larger manuscript that turned out to be quite time-
consuming: an edited volume dealing with comparative political theory. The
manuscript grew out of a lecture course I had been teaching steadily for
about ten years prior to my retirement. Largely due to this text, I became
identified in the mind of many colleagues chiefly as a founder and practitioner of comparative political theory. [125]

One of the major dilemmas in Western modernity that I had not properly tackled in my previous work was the bifurcation of mind versus matter, or humanity versus nature. This dichotomy is deeply troubling, especially in light of the mounting evidence of global warming and the growing devastation of natural resources. It so happened that, in late 2009, a major international conference on climate change was held in Copenhagen. As a corollary or adjunct of that conference, a smaller academic meeting on ecology and human nature was convened at the University of Aarhus in Denmark, and I was invited to participate. My interest and even eagerness to participate was further stimulated by two events at the time: the passing away of the ecological thinker and activist Thomas Berry in 2009 and of the "ecosophist" Raimon Panikkar in 2010. At the meeting in Aarhus I paid tribute to Berry for his portrayal of nature as "sacred liturgy," while also endorsing Panikkar's nondualist and "cosmotheandric" vision of the world.[126]

Prompted by these experiences, I decided to undertake a longer study devoted to the possible reconciliation or healing of the rift between humanity and nature. As I realized clearly, the remedy could not be found in simple human self-erasure or an atavistic plunge into "naturalism"; instead of promoting reconciliation, this plunge would result in the truncation or amputation of distinctive human qualities (like consciousness and agency). The question hence became how these qualities could be rethought and reconceived in such a fashion as to be compatible with a notion of nature as a comprehensive matrix of life. As I discovered, I was not alone in undertaking such an inquiry. Proceeding in my study, I noticed that there actually is a kind of submerged history or counterhistory accompanying the dominant Western humanity/nature split. The line of thinking on which I came to concentrate led me from Spinoza's equation of nature with "divine substance" to Schelling's idealist philosophy of nature, and from there to the great celebrations of nature by Romantic thinkers and poets, to Dewey's and Merleau-Ponty's recovery of nature's role in ordinary and "life-world" experience, and finally to Heidegger's reconnection of nature and being, both seen as self-revealing and self-sheltering sources of life. As a kind of afterthought, I added reflections on the status of nature in Asian thought—from Hinduism and Buddhism to Taoism and Confucianism—where the preferred orientation is to link nature with the "way" (*tao*). The study was finally published as *Return to Nature? An Ecological Counterhistory* (2011).[127]

ARAB SPRING, RUSSIA, ASIA

While I was working to overcome rifts, the world was moving pretty much in the opposite direction. Like many similar gatherings, the climate conference in Copenhagen ended without producing any tangible results. Moreover, longstanding geopolitical rivalries continued to fester and even intensify. Above all, September 11 continued to cast its long shadows, mainly in the form of Islamophobia and related cultural-religious animosities. At a time when cross-cultural studies celebrated the rise of a "borderless" world, geo-politics asserted itself in the form of new borders, new fences, and the hard-ening of friend-enemy demarcations. In December of 2010, the Arab Spring started in Tunisia with the self-immolation of a protester and soon spread from there to Egypt, Yemen, Libya, and other parts of the Near East. Given the otherwise dark global scenario, the Arab Spring was greeted with joy by many progressive people hoping that the events signaled the end of en-trenched autocracies. Hopes of this kind seemed initially well founded. To a large extent, the rebellion was successful in Tunisia, and for a time also in Egypt. However, soon geopolitical realities conspired to overwhelm and crush the seeds of freedom and self-government in many Muslim countries.

In my view, the change from "spring" to "winter" can be dated quite accurately: it started with the turn to wholesale violence accompanied by Western military intervention in Libya in mid-2011. In talking with some liberal friends, I was amazed by the naive trust placed in the beneficence of Western powers, despite their colonial and imperialist ventures in the past. This miscalculation exacted a price and continues to do so to the present day. I am firmly convinced that democracy can only be won by indigenous people themselves—and should preferably be won by nonviolent means. As Arendt correctly stated, echoing Gandhi, "Violence does indeed change the world— into a more violent world" (not a more democratic one).[128]

What made the descent into winter dangerous for the rest of the world were the geopolitical overtones of Near Eastern conflicts. As I see it, con-flicts in that area are, to a large extent, offshoots or proxies of geopolitical strategies—strategies that seem to point relentlessly in the direction of a renewed Cold War (and possibly World War III). Starting in 2011, one of the flashpoints of this scenario has been Syria. However, behind that flashpoint is the larger issue of Iran. Even before the Arab Spring, propaganda for a war against Iran had been strong in the West; the recent turbulence and near-chaos in parts of the Near East emboldened proponents of this propaganda by (seemingly) increasing the chances of success. Needless to say, these war drums are an offense to peace-loving people—especially those attracted to the "dialogue among civilizations." Moreover, modern wars are incredibly destructive (as Iraq has shown); and no civilized person would wish this destruction on any country, least of all on a country like Iran whose culture has bestowed on humanity splendid gifts: in philosophy, literature, music, poetry, and the arts.[129]

Beyond Iran, the simmering Cold War II mentality extends to Eastern countries, especially Russia and China. After the dismantling of the Soviet Union, attitudes in the West toward Russia—now the Russian Federation—

have not greatly changed. The only thing that is appreciated is the period of perestroika when the country was suddenly opened to Western markets and the blessings of financial capitalism. That, at some earlier time, the country also was home to a Pushkin, Tolstoy, and Dostoevsky—on the far side of both capitalism and Soviet totalitarianism—tends to be forgotten. Given its long history and accomplishments, the country is proud of its hard-won independence in the struggle against fascism and unwilling to surrender it to geopolitical machinations. Although not an expert in that history, my interest in global dialogue has also brought me closer to Russia. Soon after September 11, in 2002, I joined a new international organization called World Public Forum—Dialogue of Civilizations, which involves people from all walks of life and from all parts of the world, but where Russians play an important role (the founding president, Vladimir Yakunin, is Russian). Registered as an INGO in Vienna, the Forum held until 2015 large annual meetings in Rhodes, Greece, to consider and discuss major global problems, with discussions ranging from geopolitical, economic, and environmental to cultural and religious issues.[130]

Apart from the Russian angle, some of the animus of geopolitical rivalry, though perhaps to a lesser extent, is directed against mainland China—another country with a distinguished history and fiercely protective of its independence (after the foreign interventions during World War II and the earlier period of unequal treaties). My own relation with China comes mainly through Confucianism to which I had first been introduced by my friends Tu Weiming, Roger Ames, and Henry Rosemont in Hawaii. Although formally a communist country, China in recent decades has encouraged liberal market activities as well as the retrieval and cultivation of its own philosophical and spiritual traditions as an antidote to rampant materialism and rapacious individualism.

This retrieval is illustrated by this personal anecdote. I was fortunate to be invited to one of the very first mainland conferences on Confucius held in Nanjing in 1994. Although organized by party officials, I was amazed by the genuine fondness for Confucian teachings among academics and other people in the audience. To my delight, my hosts made it possible for me to visit the home and the tomb of Confucius in Qufu and also to travel to the top of the holy mountain Tai-shan nearby. My attachment to the sage of Qufu was firmly planted at that time. While still in Nanjing, I asked my hosts whether I could perhaps visit a temple or monastery at some distance from the city where, according to legend, Lao Tzu had spent some years. My hosts were surprised and a bit taken aback because (as they told me) visitors usually just wanted to see the new factories and industries and nobody had ever asked to see that temple. We traveled by car to the place located in wooded hills, and I discovered to my amazement that the temple was well maintained by a group of faithful Taoist monks. Toward evening, when it was beginning to get dark,

Tomb of Confucius in Qufu, Shandon Province, China; Dennis Cox/Alamy Stock Photo.

we decided to return to the city but stopped along the way in a small village where we heard chanting. Following that sound, we discovered another temple where a group of Buddhist monks and villagers had assembled for evening service. Thus, on that one visit over twenty years ago, I discovered that, despite rapid modernization, China is a country with a rich culture, an ample heart, and a spirit quite hospitable to a humanist like me.

My visit to Nanjing was the first, but fortunately not the last journey to China. During the first decade of the present century, I traveled repeatedly to China, usually for a combination of lectures and sightseeing explorations. In this manner, I visited Beijing, Shanghai, Xian, and other places. Once, start-

Tu Weiming, Chinese philosopher; Director of Institute for Advanced Studies in Humanism in Beijing.

ing out from Nepal, I took a guided tour through Tibet that led me to Potala Palace in Lhasa and many other famous sites. At another time, after attending a conference in Hong Kong, I traveled from there north to Canton or Guangzhou (with its Sunyatsen Memorial Hall) and further to the fabulously scenic Guilin at the Li River. During this period, I deepened my relations with Confucian experts, especially with Tu Weiming (with whom I recorded some video conversations). I also developed close and friendly relations with the Chinese philosopher Peinim Ni and the political theorist Daniel A. Bell, who had settled in China and with whom I carried on many friendly-critical exchanges.[131]

In 2008, at a conference at Capital Normal University in Beijing, I met a young Chinese philosopher named Zhao Tingyang. We had long and animated talks during which I discovered that he was quite familiar with leading Western thinkers (like Habermas, Rawls, Rorty, Gadamer, and Derrida) but also steeped in Chinese philosophical traditions going back to the *I Ching* or "Book of Changes." We decided to collaborate on a book dealing with recent philosophical developments and debates in China. The result was *Contemporary Chinese Political Thought: Perspectives and Debates* (2012), a book that shows the curious coexistence and correlation of Western-style liberalism, New Leftism, and Confucianism in China today.[132] I should add that, at the time when we assembled this book, I had the good fortune of being invited several times to Seoul, Korea, and especially to Kyung Hee University, which annually organizes an international Peace Festival. Many friendships were either rekindled or freshly initiated at these meetings. What particularly struck me in Seoul was the combination of a genuine Confucian mentality with a generous liberality and world-openness that, in my view, can serve as a beacon for our world.[133]

COSMOPOLITANISM AND NEW HORIZONS

Since 2010 the global horizon has darkened steadily. Given the grim global scenario, I considered it an intellectual and moral obligation to reaffirm the solidarity of humanity in the face of geopolitical and extremist-religious propaganda. Hence, I embarked on a study of cosmopolitanism, not just in the legal and institutional but the broader cultural and philosophical sense. The first step needed along this path was to overcome the Cartesian bifurcation between self and others, between the *cogito* and the world outside of it. To make some headway in this area, I enlisted again Heidegger's construal of human being (*Dasein*) as "being-in-the-world," where world or worldhood is not an alien terrain but rather co-constitutive of human being itself. As one should note, the connection of human being and world in this view is not a static or fixed structure but is permeated by temporality; hence, human being-in-the-world is constantly "temporalized" in the direction of future possibilities. At a closer look I came to realize that this view is not far removed from Deweyan pragmatism as well as from Alfred North Whitehead's process philosophy. What emerges from these insights is the notion of a "becoming world" and also of a "becoming cosmopolis" beckoning from the future as a possibility and a promise.

Transferring these considerations to ongoing discussions of "cosmopolitanism," I distinguished between three meanings of that term: first, a purely factual empirical meaning involving economic and technological globalization, that is, the spatial extension of markets, technical gadgets, and information networks; second, a normative sense referring to the rules of international law and their institutional embodiment in a legal world order; and last, a practical meaning pointing to the need for concrete engagements across national, cultural, and religious boundaries. In my view, given the enormous constraints imposed by *Realpolitik* and modern technology, the latter meaning is of primary significance for the building of a pluralistic and dialogical cosmopolis.

Once cosmopolis is seen as a mutually engaged and solicitous community—though making room for broad cultural diversity—several preconditions of cosmopolitan life come clearly into view. One is the need for a measure of social-economic equality, the latter interpreted in the sense of equal dignity, equality of respect, and equality of life chances. In this respect, the extension of neoliberalism and "vulture capitalism" into the global arena has led to forms of economic inequality and rampant exploitation that a United Nations report once described as having reached "grotesque proportions." The financial meltdown of 2008–2009 had demonstrated the grim consequences of economic inequality and class divisions for cosmopolitan life. Another major prerequisite for this life is the provision and improvement of educational opportunities around the globe. Especially when started at an early age, education can foster the cultivation of responsible civic dispositions, both on the domestic and the supranational level, and hence contribute to the growth of something like "world citizenship" (as philosopher Martha Nussbaum has so eloquently argued).[134] On both domestic and global levels, education is also urgently needed to combat the media-induced ignorance or amnesia regarding ecological devastation and the ultimate exhaustibility of natural resources.

Given the worldwide, sometimes violent upsurge of religion in public life, a question that demanded to be addressed was the place of secularism in our times. It so happens that Charles Taylor not long ago published a major tome titled *A Secular Age,* which rightly gained wide attention and which, critiquing modernization as the denial of theistic transcendence, pleaded for the revival of the latter. This book prompted me to consult a parallel volume by Raimon Panikkar titled *The Rhythm of Being,* which (in a more Heideggerian vein) portrays modern secularity as pointing to the potential overcoming of the "transcendence-immanence" conundrum—a portrayal more congenial to my own nondualistic (*Advaita*) inclinations. At the same time, I entered the debate about "postsecularity" launched by Habermas, bending this term ultimately in the direction of an ethically and spiritually nurtured cosmopolitan commitment. After adding some reflections on contemporary developments in the Muslim world, my cosmopolitan book was published as *Being in the World: Dialogue and Cosmopolis* (2013).[135]

It goes without saying that cosmopolitan reflections of this kind are futile if the only reality to be taken into account is the present, that is, if we ignore the temporality of "being-in-the-world" and the possibility of future horizons. As it had become increasingly clear to me, an opening to such horizons

Raimon Panikkar, Spanish/Indian philosopher-theologian; University of Santa Barbara, USA; Agence Opale/Alamy Stock Photo.

requires not just a change of individual attitudes but a change of the entire modern paradigm or frame of significance, that is, of our mode of "bring-in-the-world."[136] Perhaps the most metaphysically encrusted category of Western modernity is the concept of freedom, which, although initially endowed with a liberating élan, over time congealed into a dogmatically asserted privilege and possession. Anchored in a fixed subject and seen as exclusionary property, the category of freedom necessarily stands opposed to the outside world and especially to any form of social solidarity—an antimony that surfaced with a vengeance in the Cold War divide between the "Free World" and Marxist socialism. Any attempt to deconstruct this antimony, it became clear to me, requires a rigorous rethinking of the polar categories as used in modern political thought. Important guideposts for such a rethinking are provided once again in Heidegger's work, where freedom is portrayed not as an exclusionary property but rather as an openness to the unfolding horizons of truth challenging us to find our way in the world. Seen in this light, solidarity is not the opposite, but rather the intimate corollary of our living freely in the world. To be sure, Heidegger is not alone in having pinpointed this correlation of freedom and solidarity. In many ways, his insight was anticipated by Dewey in his presentation of modern democracy as an ethical community of free people. Among more recent political thinkers, Hannah Arendt has been exemplary in her rethinking of crucial concepts like freedom, authority, and tradition. [137]

The effort to reconnect freedom and solidarity is theoretically challenging but even more so—and sometimes nearly impossible—in the practical-political domain. Due to the modern growth of a massive state apparatus, on the one hand, and the progressive atomization of social life, on the other, the ethical bond that is supposed to link a public community together is bound to be stretched, sometimes to the breaking point. This point is reached when public elites—especially the modern super-Leviathan—seek to subject a population to near-total control, thereby stifling the voice of conscience and preventing individuals (or groups) from speaking truth to power. In this situation—often captured in the phrase "man versus the state"—the freedom-solidarity nexus is ruptured, making room instead for a polar antimony likely to result in violence or death. The situation has been the focus of a large and inspiring literature, a literature that has gained dramatic relevance in recent times under the aegis of the security and surveillance state (and should be required reading in civic education courses). Most famous in this genre are Henry David Thoreau's text "Civil Disobedience" and Albert Camus's *The Rebel*.

History, both ancient and modern, is replete with instructive examples of this antimony—from the conflict between Antigone and the king of Thebes and the condemnation of Socrates by the Athenian jury to the execution of Thomas More by Henry VIII. However, the most gripping examples are provided by the struggles against modern totalitarianism, especially the German resistance against the Nazi regime, epitomized by the activities of the White Rose organization and the circle around Count Stauffenberg and Pastor Bonhoeffer. All these considerations weighed heavily on me when I embarked on a new book project: a project presenting the correlation of freedom and solidarity as a paradigm shift. The project proved to be arduous and was by no means facilitated by prevailing political conditions.

IN THE DARKNESS, LIGHT A CANDLE

Unhappily, in the ensuing years geopolitical conditions in the world deteri-
orated steadily. One aspect was the worsening of relations between the West
and Russia and hence the intensification of the new Cold War (epitomized by
the events in the Ukraine and the advance of NATO to Russia's borders). At
the same time, total chaos spread in the Middle East, mainly due to the rise of
the Islamic State (ISIS), leading to steadily more brutal terror wars and proxy
wars in the region and the world as a whole. These wars in turn triggered a
huge and seemingly endless flood of migrants seeking refuge in presumably
more stable and peaceful regions of the world. In response to this refugee
crisis, something was awakened in many countries that had been dormant for
many decades: the contagion of nationalism, chauvinism, and xenophobia
(sometimes bordering on fascism). Thus, calls went out in many areas for the
toughening of border controls and even for the closure of borders and the
erection of walls and fences between peoples. What seemed to be emerging
was a global Hobbesian scenario, a picture of the world as a global battlefield. When combined with chauvinism (and protofascism), this picture
evoked some of the worst memories of my early childhood.

Faced with these developments—the butchery of hundreds of thousands
of people, the massive homelessness, and the looming threat of a global
nuclear disaster—I was nearly driven into the pit of despair. As it happened,
the geopolitical malaise was compounded for me by a series of personal
traumas. In the midst of the global turmoil I was struggling with cancer
which, as I mentioned, involved a long series of treatments and procedures.
At some point during these procedures I suffered a severe breakdown that
shook me to the core of my being. It was clear that I had to disengage myself
from some of my commitments. Above all, I realized the wisdom of my
earlier decision to retire—in stages—from my university position.

After about two years, my cancer was pronounced to be in remission,
which restored to my life a sense of stability. In addition to physical stability,
I also gained some greater personal clarity. As I came to see, the mentioned
traumas were not just debilitating but also enabling in the sense of engender-
ing a learning experience. Maybe (I came to think) the traumas afflicted me
in a salutary way to rid me of a still lingering egocentrism or anthropocentrism—a delusion which obscured for me the point of my life's endeavors.
What dawned upon me—at first only inchoately—was that perhaps my life's
journey and all my endeavors were nothing but a gloss on a single word in
the Lord's prayer: *adveniat*, "may it come." We know that what is prayerful-
ly solicited to come is *regnum tuum*, "your reign"—which is not "my" nor
even "our" reign, but rather "your" reign with us (or our reign under your
guidance). Such a reign or "kingdom," I became convinced, cannot be purely
clerical nor purely secular; it cannot be purely "transcendental" nor "imma-

nent." Also, the reign cannot be merely for some people or some culture or some churches. Rather it must be for all—embracing all cultures and traditions, and even nonbelievers. Thus, the reign has to be *kat-holon,* "for the whole"—where the "whole" is not a substance but a *polyhedron* allowing for a multitude of differences and even for absences and the "unknown."

Seen from this perspective (which I adopt not as a fact but only as a hope), I am really nobody, and my life's story is about nobody but someone who was sent "on the way." As a friend once told me, the spirit uses tricks to guide us. In my case, it seems the spirit used some native inclinations to send me "into the world": my inborn curiosity, my love of traveling, my delight in unfamiliar landscapes, peoples, and cultures. But from the beginning (I can say) my excursions were never undertaken for mere touristic enjoyment or self-gratification. Somehow, behind the array of unfamiliar or exotic appearances, I was always searching for something: call it the possibility or the promise of peace with justice—which is just another expression for *regnum tuum.* In scripture, we are exhorted to "seek your face" (*faciem tuam requiram*)—which is nothing but the radiant face of (transcognitive) truth, goodness, and justice. Without this search or quest, everything I have done or written crumbles into dust.

In terms of my academic work, the described traumas and experiences unleashed an upsurge of scholarly endeavor. After hovering for some time at the edge of despair, I decided that dejection was pointless: it was time to light candles in the darkness. This decision explains the publication in rapid succession of a number of books. The first was meant to be a wake-up call: to stir myself and my contemporaries up from complacency and the mind-numbing coma induced by incessant noise-mongering and war-mongering. Titled *Mindfulness and Letting Be: On Engaged Thinking and Acting* (2014), the book was intended as a summons to sober reflection and a readiness to "think what we are doing" (Arendt). One of my next books was even more direct and urgent in its appeal: *Against Apocalypse: Holding the World Together* (2016). The text was a protest against an idea that was increasingly circulating in the global corridors of power: the idea that nuclear war might somehow be "winnable." The book was preceded by the completion of another project that was designed to tone down raging culture wars, especially the steadily intensifying Cold War between West and East, *Freedom and Solidarity: Toward New Beginnings* (2015)—where "new beginnings" intimates a basic paradigm shift.

The year 2016 was particularly hard and stressful. Apart from geopolitical rivalries and a poisoned election climate in America, the year brought to an end my service as co-chair of the international World Public Forum—Dialogue of Civilizations. To commemorate the decade-long work of that Forum, my friend Edward Demenchonok and myself assembled a number of outstanding papers presented at the Forum's last meeting. Its title—*A World*

Beyond Global Disorder: The Courage to Hope—was a remonstration against the widespread climate of looming disaster. With some delay (due mainly to the international cast of contributors), the book was published in 2017. The same year also witnessed the publication of two new books: *Democracy to Come: Politics as Relational Praxis* and *Spiritual Guides: Pathfinders in the Desert*. The first book was another elaboration on the meaning of *adveniat*—now on the level of a global democracy with an accent on the ethical equality of peoples. The second book testifies to the fact that the "coming reign" cannot just be a humanly manufactured "our reign," but requires spiritual guidance by pathfinders in the present desert. The chief pathfinders chosen for the book are Paul Tillich, Raimon Panikkar, Thomas Merton, and Pope Francis. I am still working on a third book, which will be called *Beyond (Neo-)Liberalism: Toward a Social and Democratic Commonwealth*, a title which is another gloss on *regnum tuum*.

A PRELIMINARY FAREWELL

At this point, having recounted in broad outline the story of my life, it seems appropriate to return to the beginning and to acknowledge, once again, the many contexts and relationships in which my story has always been embedded. Looking back, I find that none of the steps of my life have ever been the result of utterly autonomous choice or free decision—although I certainly cannot blame any of these steps on external forces or conditions. As it seems to me, the course of my life has been guided mostly by hunches, cues, or intuitions—cues that initially were hard to decipher. Only in retrospect did some of the steps disclose a certain directedness and intelligible sense—the latter being a mixture of reasoning and sensibility (or sensuality). For example, my frequent trips to India were due only in part to intellectual curiosity, the desire to learn from philosophical *darshanas*; in good (perhaps major) part they were enticed by sounds, smells, lights, faces, gestures (*mudras*), and amorphous longings nearly impossible to pinpoint. The same is true of my frequent visits to Nepal where the desire for clarity seems to be mocked by innumerable monkeys inhabiting temple grounds. And what is one to say of the temple cities of South India, those temples within temples, where intelligible storytelling is drowned in a veritable cornucopia of stories assembled on towering *gopurams*?

Looking at these *gopurams*, one realizes how intimately one's life is embroiled with other stories without which it could not have happened or be what it is. This realization is sobering and salutary. Taking it to heart, the final phase of one's life should be marked not by ill will or bitterness, but by gratitude—gratitude toward one's fellow human beings, toward nature's gifts, and toward the ground (or un-ground) that nurtures and sustains everything. In my case, gratitude is due, first of all, to my parents who raised me, in extremely difficult circumstances, with unfailing love, sensitivity, and forbearance for my escapades (including my emigration to a far-off land). More than their words, it was their good example that provided some steadiness to my life. Infinite gratitude is due also to my wife Ilse who became my steady companion in my new homeland ever since my late twenties. What I find particularly noteworthy is that our loving symbiosis always left room for development on both sides; without estrangement, there was always a healthy balance between togetherness and freedom, between dependence and independence—without which my far-flung cosmopolitan adventures would have been impossible. We have been blessed with two children, a girl and a boy, who have brought untold joy into our live—including the joy of grandchildren. Next to my direct family I am grateful to the companion of my youth, Robert, with whom I have been linked in steady friendship for some seventy-five years. This has been that rare kind of relationship that persists and even grows without the need of elaborate explanation: even after a longer period of separation one instantly knows the other's condition before uttering a word.

In the course of recounting my life story, I have mentioned the names of many other people to whom I am grateful: teachers of my youth and my adult life, and friends and colleagues in many parts of the world. I shall not repeat their names here; I trust my story conveys the sense of felt gratitude (many of these names are also cited in the various prefaces to my books). All these human relationships, of course, could not be maintained without the blessings of nature's bounty—which renders imperative the fostering of ecological responsibility. Actually, in my view, nature is not just an "environment," but is part of us and penetrates into our being. What this penetration brings into view is the broader web of things, the infinitely rich and varied source of all beings—a source for which we have no definition or agreed upon name but which gratitude impels us to cherish and to venerate. Without confessional narrowness or definitional scruples, my life story is simply a little tributary which, coming from somewhere, ultimately flows into that vast ocean which, in the end, gives meaning (or un-meaning) to its course and toward which it is simply another *itinerarium (mentis in Deum)*.[138]

NOTES

1. Marcel Proust, *Swann in Love*, trans. C. K. Scott Moncrieff and Trent Kilmartin (New York: Vintage Books, 1984), pp. 265–266.

2. Proverbs 4:23. The passage served as an inscription over the door of Martin Heidegger's house in Freiburg-Zähringen.

3. Gabriel Marcel, *The Mystery of Being*, 2 vols., trans. G. S. Fraser and René Hague (London: Harvill Press, 1951/1960).

4. See Nicolaus of Cusa, *Idiota de Sapientia – Der Laie über die Weisheit*, ed. Ronate Steiger (Hamburg: Felix Meiner, 1988); and *De docta ignorantia – Die belehrte Unwissenheit*, ed. Hans G. Singer (Hamburg: Felix Meiner, 1944). Compare also my "Wise Ignorance: Nicolaus of Cusa's Search for Truth," in *In Search of the Good Life: A Pedagogy for Troubled Times* (Lexington, NY: University of Kentucky Press, 2007), pp. 58–79. The phrase "I search for your face" (*faciem tuam requiram*) is found in Psalm 27:8.

5. Cicero, *De senectude, De amicitia, De divinatione,* Latin-English, trans. William A. Falconer (Cambridge, MA: Harvard University Press, 2001), p. 15.

6. Norberto Bobbio, *Old Age and Other Essays*, trans. Allan Cameron (Cambridge, UK: Polity Press, 2001), pp. 8, 13–14.

7. *Old Age and Other Essays*, p. 12. He adds a passage which, in my view, captures the haunting quality of old age (p. 13): "When in your memory you turn to places of the past, the dead crowd around you, and their number increases with every passing year. You have been abandoned by the majority of those whose company you kept. But you cannot cancel them from your memory as though they had never existed. When you recall them to your mind, you bring them back to life, at least for a moment, and they are no longer entirely dead—they have not disappeared completely into nothing: the friend who died as a teenager in a climbing accident or the school friend whose plane crashed during the war, whose body was never found and whose return his family expected for many years."

8. Confucius, *Analects* 2:4.

9. Johann Wolfang Goethe, "Marienbader Elegie," *Sämtliche Werke* (Frankfurt: Deutscher Klassiker Verlag, 1988), Abteilung I, volume 2, pp. 457–462. Elsewhere, the same poet wrote: "Ich besass es doch einmal, was so köstlich ist. Dass man doch zu seiner Qual, nimmer es vergisst!" See "An den Mond," *ibid.*, 66. Here, then, is the ambivalence of memories: they can be delightful, but also the source of torment.

10. Paul Ricoeur, *Vivant jusqu'a la Mort; suivi de Fragments* (Paris: Ediitons du Seuil, 2007), p. 76.

11. See Gabriel Marcel, *Homo Viator: Introduction to a Metaphysic of Hope*, trans. Emma Craufurd (New York: Harper & Row, 1962), p. 239.

12. I might also mention that, since the Middle Ages, Augsburg has been divided into an "upper" and a "lower" city. In earlier times, the upper city was inhabited mainly by clergy and nobility, the lower city by workers and servants. Later on, the upper city become home to merchants and business people, the lower city to workers and artisans (like goldsmiths, silversmiths, and jewellers). Since my father was a realtor and hence a businessman, we lived in the upper part near the city hall; but I have always felt equally at home in both parts. The writer Berthold Brecht was born and grew up in the lower city where there is now an impressive museum in his honor.

13. I have read somewhere, regarding a French writer: "He suffered all his life from a happy childhood." The statement could not be applied to me.

14. Confucius, *Analects*, 4:18.

15. See *The Adages of Erasmus*, selected by William Barker (Toronto: University of Toronto Press, 2001), pp. 317–356 (Adage IV, 1).

16. During this time, French theater troupes would often perform in Augsburg. I remember vividly how the actor Gérard Philippe visited the city and how I was awestruck by his talent. Another time Jean Cocteau came with a company and dazzled our young imagination. (I must have seen his film *Orphée* at least three or four times.) Generally, in the young German population there was an immense appetite for everything French—something, I believe, which aided in the reconciliation between the two countries later engineered by such leaders as Robert Schuman and Konrad Adenauer.

17. Recently I was reading some writings by Thich Nhat Hanh, the Vietnamese Buddist monk. He vigorously challenges the assumption that Buddhism can be reduced to the formula: "All is suffering." The real point is to move beyond suffering. See, e.g., his *The Heart of the Buddha's Teaching: Transforming Suffering into Peace, Joy, and Liberation* (New York: Broadway Books, 1999).

18. Together with several other members of the community Mishkin subsequently emigrated to Australia. On the topic of music I should add: I was also very fond of singing during that

period. In fact, I sang simultaneously in youth choirs, church choirs, and large city choirs. For a time I was also the conductor of a small youth choir (where we performed mostly madrigals and folks songs).

19. Endowed with great dexterity, my brother was really good at carpenting. Occasionally he would remind me that Jesus too had been a carpenter—to my considerable annoyance.

20. On the lighter side, there is this story. In Riedlingen there was a cousin, Mechthilde, who was a very spirited young woman. One time she enticed me to travel by train all the way from Riedlingen to Augsburg—dressed as a girl. As I was told, I was not bad-looking—but my mother was really taken aback on my arrival.

21. Although formally enrolled at the University of Munich, I spent a semester at the University of Erlangen (which was possible under an agreement between Bavarian universities). By comparison with Munich, Erlangen is a more provincial town; it is also preponderantly Protestant. I do not recall much about my courses there. Animated by classmates, I frequented some fraternities there. Although enjoying the cameraderie, I was repelled by the excessive beer drinking. Later I learned that some fraternities had resumed the practice of dueling—which, to me, is the height of "macho" stupidity.

22. Somehow, I had the impression that Schmitt was even unfamiliar with that part of Hobbes's work. Since I was just a young student, I did not press the issue; but somehow I had the feeling of an important difference of interpretation. See Schmitt, *Ex Captivitate Salus* (Cologne: Greven, 1950); *Donoso Cortés in gesamteuropäischer Interpretation* (Cologne: Greven, 1950); *Der Nomos der Erde im Völkerrecht des Jus Publicus Europaeum* (Cologne: Greven, 1950). The last book has been translated into English as *The Nomos of the Earth in the International Law of the Jus Publicum Europaeum*, trans. G. L. Ulmen (New York: Telos Press, 2003). Compare also my "Epimeteo Cristiano o Prometeo Pagano" *Revista Internazionale de Filosofia del Diritto*, vol. 35 (1958), pp. 657–679.

23. Compare in this regard my essay (written much later) "The Law of Peoples: Civilizing Humanity" in *Peace Talks—Who Will Listen?* (Notre Dame, IN: University of Notre Dame, 2004), pp. 42–63.

24. In Brussels, I first lived in a residence hall of the university but later rented a room with a family in the city. My move into that home seemed to occasion some tension in the family. A fierce Francophile, the husband apparently considered the presence of a young German in their midst provocative or obnoxious—a sentiment luckily not shared by his wife. Once I overheard an animated debate on that issue, an altercation which the wife managed to resolve in my favor.

25. Among other pieces I wrote an essay titled "*Um ein Europa von innen bittend*" (Begging for a Europe from Within). The essay was inspired by Ortega y Gasset's famous essay "*Um einen Goethe von einen bittend*" which tried to rescue Goethe from his Olympian pedestal and make him available for ordinary people. See Gasset, *Triptico: Mirabeau, o El politico; Kant; Goethe desde dentro* (Madrid: Espasa-Calpe, 1964).

26. One of my earliest published essays dealt with Bobbio. See "Studie über Norberto Bobbio," *Archiv für Rechts- und Sozialphilosophie*, vol. 42 (1956), pp. 403–428. In conversation, Bobbio called Kelsen one of his own early mentors. Later he published his book *Diritto e potere: saggi su Kelsen* (Naples: Edizioni Scientifiche Italiani, 1992). Like Schmitt, Bobbio was strongly interested in Thomas Hobbes; but what he valued was not the latter's voluntarism and stress on sovereign power, but his rational lucidity. He would certainly not have appreciated my interest in Heidegger—which, however, emerged later. Curiously, during the later part of the century, Turin University became the home of a Heideggerian philosopher and democrat, Gianni Vattimo (who eventually also became a friend).

27. I take this information from Bobbio's "The Politics of Culture" in *Old Age and Other Essays*, pp. 91–93.

28. *Old Age and Other Essays*, 92.

29. All these writings, comprising the "Early," "Middle" and "Later" works, were published in 37 volumes by Southern Illinois University Press between 1969 and 1990. Still later, Southern Illinois University became the academic home of two leading Dewey scholars: Larry Hickman and Thomas Alexander.

30. See Fred Dallmayr and Robert S. Rankin, *Freedom and Emergency Power, in the Cold War* (New York: Appleton-Century-Crofts, 1964).

31. At the time of writing my thesis, Hannah Arendt's famous study of the two revolutions had not yet appeared. See *On Revolution* (New York: Viking Press, 1965). After the publication of that text, my desire to return to my earlier thesis was further diminished.

32. Compare in this context Calvin Schrag, *Existence and Freedom: Towards an Ontology of Human Freedom* (Evanston, IL: Northwestern University Press, 1961); *Experience and Being: Prolegomena to a Future Ontology* (Evanston, IL: Northwestern University Press, 1969); and among his later writings, *God as Otherwise than Being: Toward a Semantics of the Gift* (Evanston, IL: Northwestern University Press, 2002). Compare also Ralph William Vunderink, *The Nature of Being in the Thought of Paul Tillich and Martin Heidegger* (Chicago: University of Chicago Press, 1969); and Thomas F. O'Meara, "Tillich and Heidegger: A Structural Relationship," *Harvard Theological Review*, vol. 61 (1968), pp. 249–261.

33. See, e.g., John Sallis, *Echoes: After Heidegger* (Bloomington, IN: Indiana University Press, 1990); *Phenomenology and the Return to Beginnings* (Pittsburgh: Duquesne University Press, 1973); Babette E. Babich, ed., *From Phenomenology to Thought: Essays in Honor of William J. Richardson* (Boston: Kluwer Academic, 1995); Theodore J. Kisiel, *The Genesis of Heidegger's Being and Time* (Berkeley, CA: University of California Press, 1993); *Heidegger's Way of Thought* (New York: Continuum, 2001); John D. Caputo, *Demythologizing Heidegger* (Bloomington, IN: Indiana University Press, 1993); *Radical Hermeneutics* (Bloomington, IN: Indiana University Press, 1987); Merold Westphal, *God, Guilt, and Death: An Existential Phenomenology of Religion* (Bloomington, IN: Indiana University Press, 1984).

34. See, e.g., Hwa Yol Jung, *Rethinking Political Theory: Essays in Phenomenology and the Study of Politics* (Athens: Ohio University Press, 1993).

35. The texts by Merleau-Ponty which influenced me most strongly at the time were *Phenomenology of Perception*, trans. Colin Smith (New York: Routledge, 1962); and *The Structure of Behavior*, trans. Alden L. Fisher (Boston: Beacon Press, 1963).

36. C. P. Snow, *The Two Cultures: A Second Look* (New York: Mentor Books, 1964).

37. See my "Political Science and the Two Cultures," in *Beyond Dogma and Despair: Toward a Critical Phenomenology of Politics* (Notre Dame: University of Notre Dame Press, 1981), pp. 21–42. (The essay was first published in 1968). For Max Scheler's study see his *Die Wissensformen und die Gesellschaft* (1926; 2nd ed., Bern and Munich: Francke Verlag, 1960).

38. See my "Empirical Political Theory and the Image of Man," in *Beyond Dogma and Despair*, pp. 43–68. (The essay was first published in 1970.) Regarding Ralf Dahrendorf see his "Homo Sociologicus" and "Sociology and Human Nature" in his *Essays in the Theory of Society* (Stanford, CA: Stanford University Press, 1968). Regarding Harold D. Lasswell see *Psychopathology and Politics* (Chicago University Press, 1930; rev. ed. New York: Viking Press, 1960); and *Power and Personality* (New York: Norton, 1948; rev. ed. New York: Viking Press, 1962). Regarding "exchange" models compare James M. Buchanan and Gordon Tullock, *The Calculus of Consent* (Ann Arbor: University of Michigan Press, 1962); Peter M. Blau, *Exchange and Power in Social Life* (New York: Wiley, 1964); and Anthony Downs, *An Economic Theory of Democracy* (New York: Harper & Row, 1957).

39. See my "Social Role and 'Human Nature': Plessner's Philosophical Anthropology," in *Beyond Dogma and Despair*, pp. 69–93. Compare, e.g., Helmuth Plessner, *Die Stufen des Organischen und der Mensch* (1928; 2nd ed., Berlin: Walter de Grugter, 1965); *Conditio Humana* (Pfullingen: Neske, Verlag, 1964); *Philosophische Anthropologie* (Bonn: Bouvier Verlag, 1967). Compare also Arnold Gehlen, *Der Mensch: Seine Natur und Seine Stellung in der Welt* (1940; 8th ed., Bonn: Athenäum Verlag, 1966); *Urmensch und Spätkultur* (Bonn: Athenäum Verlag, 1956). Regarding Scheler see his *Die Stellung des Menschen im Kosmos* (Bern: Francke Verlag, 1927).

40. See my "Phenomenology and Social Science: An Overview and Appraisal," in *Beyond Dogma and Despair*, pp. 97–119. Compare also Alfred Schutz, *The Phenomenology of the Social World*, trans. George Walsh and Frederick Lehnert (Evanston, IL: Northwestern University Press, 1967).

41. Fred Dallmayr and Thomas A. McCarthy, eds., *Understanding and Social Inquiry* (Notre Dame, IN: University of Notre Dame Press, 1977).

42. After leaving Purdue, I wrote an essay on Strauss in which I attempted to give a somewhat balanced assessment. See "Leo Strauss Peregrinus," *Social Research*, vol. 61 (1994),

pp. 877–906. Regarding Thomas Hobbes, by the way, I believe Strauss made a mistake by attributing the social contract to a shared "fear of death"—when the actual Hobbesian motive is "fear of violent death." Although we cannot avoid death, we can at least try to minimize the danger of violent death. See Strauss, *The Political Philosophy of Thomas Hobbes, Its Basis and Its Genesis*, trans. Elsa M. Sinclair (Chicago: University of Chicago Press, 1952). Compare also his *What is Political Philosophy? and Other Studies* (Chicago: University of Chicago Press, 1959/1988); and my "Strauss and the 'Moral Basis' of Thomas Hobbes," *Archiv für Rechts-und Sozialphilosophie*, vol. 52 (1966), pp. 25–66.

43. The relation between Strauss and political neo-conservatism is highly controverted. The relation is particularly complicated by Strauss' tendency to retreat from "mundane" politics into a realm of "perennial ideas"—ideas which, however, were instantiated chiefly in past political arrangements. In my view, the best and most balanced account can be found in William E. Connolly's *Pluralism* (Durham, NC: Duke University Press, 2005), pp. 38–54.

44. As in the case of Strauss, I subsequently wrote an essay on Voegelin in which I tried to offer a balanced assessment (for which his widow expressed appreciation). See my "Voegelin's Search for Order," in *Margins of Political Discourse* (Albany, NY: State University of New York Press, 1989), pp. 73–94. For a slightly earlier version see "Voegelin's Search for Order," *Journal of Politics*, vol. 51 (1989), pp. 411–430.

45. See Sheldon Wolin, *Politics and Vision: Continuity and Innovation in Western Political Thought* (Boston, MA: Little, Brown & Co., 1960). Compare also his later *Democracy Incorporated: Managed Democracy and the Specter of Inverted Totalitarianism* (Princeton, NJ: Princeton University Press, 2008).

46. See William E. Connolly, *Appearance and Reality in Politics* (New York: Cambridge University Press, 1981); *Political Theory and Modernity* (New York: Blackwell, 1988); *Identity/Difference* (Ithaca, NY: Cornell University Press 1991); *The Ethos of Pluralization* (Minneapolis, MN: University of Minnesota Press, 1995); *Neuropolitics* (Minneapolis, MN: University of Minnesota Press, 2002); *A World of Becoming* (Durham, NC: Duke University Press, 2011). For a review of some of his writings see my "Connolly's Deconstruction of Modern Political Theory," *Strategies*, vol., 4/5 (1991), pp. 45–58. The intellectual diversity of the group of theorists associated with Connolly is illustrated in the series of texts titled "Modernity and Political Thought" edited by Morton Schoolman at SAGE Publications (the series was later taken over by Rowman & Littlefield). I shall return to my contribution to the series later (note 97).

47. Maurice Merleau-Ponty, *Humanism and Terror: An Essay on the Communist Problem*, trans. John O'Neill (Boston: Beacon Press, 1969), p. xxiv.

48. The strengths include the independence of research and the openness to many perspectives. Glaring weaknesses are the overcrowding of universities, the distance between teachers and students (partly due to overcrowding), and the underfunding of the social and human sciences. Some seminars I taught in Hamburg had over sixty students; lecture courses were equally overfilled.

49. Jürgen Habermas, *Erkenntnis und Interesse* (Frankfurt: Suhrkamp, Verlag, 1968); trans. by Jeremy J. Shapiro as *Knowledge and Human Interests* (Boston: Beacon Press, 1971).

50. See my "Reason and Emancipation: Notes on Habermas," *Man and World*, vol. 5 (1972), pp. 79–109; also my "Critical Theory Criticized: Habermas's *Knowledge and Human Interests* and Its Aftermath," *Philosophy of the Social Sciences*, vol. 2 (1972), pp. 211–229.

51. *Materialienband zu Habermas' Erkenntnis und Interesse*, edited with an Introduction and an Epilogue (Frankfurt: Suhrkamp Verlag, 1974).

52. Seyla Benhabib and Fred Dallmayr, *The Communicative Ethics Controversy* (Boston, MA: MIT Press, 1990).

53. Hans-Georg Gadamer, *Wahrheit und Methode: Grundzüge einer philosophischen Hermeneutik* (Tübingen: Mohr, 1960). For a good English translation see Gadamer, *Truth and Method*, 2nd rev. ed., trans. Joel Weinsheimer and Donald G. Marshall (New York: Crossroads, 1989).

54. Martin Heidegger, *Über den Humanismus* (Frankfurt: Klostermann, 1949); trans. as "Letter on Humanism" in David F. Krell, ed., *Martin Heidegger: Basic Writings* (New York: Harper & Row, 1977), pp. 193–242.

55. I should add that, following my visit to Heidelberg, I traveled to Tübingen in order to meet Ernst Bloch who, at the time, was teaching there at the university. He invited me to come to his seminar which dealt with Franz Kafka and expressivist literature. The seminar was overflowing with students, a fact which limited discussion. What I remember best was his own caustic and "expressivist" style, the twinkle in his eyes which seemed to defy difficult external circumstances (he had left East Germany a few years earlier). Several years later I wrote a tribute to him and especially his "principle of hope." See "Bloch's Principle of Hope," in *Margins of Political Discourse* (Albany, NY: State University of New York Press, 1989), pp. 158–182.

56. In this respect, Gadamer's philosophy and practical way of life were in complete harmony. To get a flavor of this harmony see *Gadamer in Conversation*, trans. Richard E. Palmer (New Haven, CT: Yale University Press, 2001).

57. Jürgen Habermas's review appeared first in *Philosophische Rundschau*, vol. 14 (1967); for an English translation see "A Review of Gadamer's *Truth and Method*," in Dallmayr and Thomas McCarthy, eds., *Understanding and Social Inquiry*, pp. 335–363.

58. For discussions of the Gadamer-Habermas debate see, e.g., my "Life-World and Critique," in *Between Freiburg and Frankfurt* (Amherst, MA: University of Massachusetts Press, 1991), pp. 13–43; Dieter Misgald, "Critical Theory and Hermeneutics: The Debate between Habermas and Gadamer," in John O'Neill, eds., *On Critical Theory* (New York: Seabury Press, 1976), pp. 164–183; and Jack Mendelson, "The Habermas-Gadamer Debate," *New German Critique*, vol. 18 (1979), pp. 44–73.

59. See my *Between Freiburg and Frankfurt: Toward a Critical Ontology* (above note 58); for a British edition see *Life-world, Modernity and Critique: Paths between Heidegger and the Frankfurt School* (Cambridge, UK: Polity Press, 1991).

60. An effort to "split the difference" had been made by Paul Ricoeur in his "Hermeneutics and the Critique of Ideology," in *Hermeneutics and the Human Sciences*, ed. and trans., John B. Thompson (Cambridge, UK: Cambridge University Press, 1981), pp. 63–100. Compare also his *The Conflict of Interpretations: Essays in Hermeneutics*, ed. Don Ihde (Evanston, IL: Northwestern University Press, 1974). For another approach see Charles Taylor, "Interpretation and the Sciences of Man," in his *Philosophy and the Human Sciences: Philosophical Papers 2* (Cambridge, UK: Cambridge University Press, 1985), pp. 15–57; and his "Gadamer on the Human Sciences," in Robert J. Dostal, ed., *The Cambridge Companion to Gadamer* (Cambridge, UK: Cambridge University Press, 2002), pp. 126–142.

61. See in this respect Habermas, *The Theory of Communicative Action*, 2 vols., trans. Thomas McCarthy (Boston: Beacon Press, 1984); *Justification and Application: Remarks on Discourse Ethics* (Cambridge, MA: MIT Press, 1993); and *Truth and Justification*, ed. and trans. Barbara Fultner (Cambridge, MA: MIT Press, 2003).

62. These notions are central to Martin Heidegger, *Sein und Zeit*, 11th ed. (Tübingen: Mohr, 1967); for an English translation see *Being and Time*, trans. John Macquarrie and Edward Robinson (New York: Harper Collins, 1962).

63. See *Twilight of Subjectivity: Contributions to a Post-Individualist Theory of Politics* (Amherst, MA: University of Massachusetts Press, 1981).

64. I am referring here especially to such texts as *Beiträge zur Philosophie (Vom Ereignis)* of 1936; *Besinnung* of 1938/39; and *Geschichte des Seyns* of 1938/40. The German texts were published first in the 1980's and 1990's; their English translation came many years later. See Heidegger, *Contributions to Philosophy (of the Event)*, trans. Richard Rojewicz and Daniela Vallega-Neu (Bloomington: Indiana University Press, 2012); *Mindfulness*, trans. Parvis Emad and Thomas Kalary (New York: Continuum, 2006).

65. I did manage to attend some of his late lectures and watch some video tapes. After his death I visited his home in Freiburg-Zähringen and also the famous "hut" in Todtnauberg. In Freiburg, one of his sons kindly took me into his study and showed me some unpublished manuscripts. I was able to sit briefly in the leather chair for guests (which in the past had been occupied by many famous people).

66. What attracted me mainly to Stuart Hampshire were his books *Thought and Action* (New York: Viking Press, 1967); *Freedom of Mind, and Other Essays* (Princeton, NJ: Princeton University of Press, 1971); *Innocence and Experience* (Cambridge, MA: Harvard University

Press, 1989). Only later did I become familiar with his work on Spinoza and Spinozism. I should add that, during my Oxford year, I established friendly relations with some colleagues in Cambridge, especially with the social theorists Anthony Giddens and David Held. With Giddens I met repeatedly at King's College, discussing his effort to establish a balance between "structure" and "agency." See especially his *Central Problems in Social Theory: Action, Structure and Contradiction in Social Analysis* (Berkeley, CA: University of California Press, 1979). For my "take" on this issue compare "Agency and Structure," *Philosophy of the Social Sciences*, vol. 12 (1982), pp. 427–438.

67. At that time I had studied with great interest his books *The Explanation of Behavior* (New York: Humanities Press, 1964); *Hegel* (Cambridge, UK: Cambridge University Press, 1975); and *Hegel and Modern Society* (Cambridge, UK: Cambridge University Press, 1979). A bit later I would study his *Sources of the Self: the Making of Modern Identity* (Cambridge, MA: Harvard University Press, 1989), and his writings on multiculturalism.

68. The only person in Oxford at that time interested in, and familiar with, French postmodern thought was Alan Montefiore—but he was and felt marginalized in his context. See his *Philosophy and Personal Relations: An Anglo-French Study* (Montreal: McGill-Queens University Press, 1973; and *Philosophy in France Today* (Cambridge, UK: Cambridge University Press, 1983).

69. The texts by Jacques Derrida important to me at the time were *Of Grammatology*, trans. Gayatri C. Spivak (Baltimore, MD: Johns Hopkins University Press, 1974); *Writing and Difference*, trans. Alan Bass (Chicago: University of Chicago Press, 1978); and *Margins of Philosophy*, trans. Alan Bass (Chicago: University of Chicago Press, 1982). The main texts by Michel Foucault were *The Order of Things: An Archaeology of the Human Sciences* (New York: Random House, 1970); *The Archaeology of Knowledge and the Discourse on Language*, trans. A. M. Sheridan Smith (New York: Pantheon Books, 1972): and *Language, Counter-Memory, Practice*, trans. Donald F. Boushard and Sherry Simon (Oxford: Blackwell, 1977). In different ways, all these books were focused on language.

70. Derrida's portrayal of "rupture" as an extraordinary intervention (or "event") probably predisposed him for a while to flirt with Carl Schmitt's stress on extra-legal "sovereignty" and still later to turn to the ethical "transcendentalism" of Emmanuel Levinas. At the time of our meeting in Paris, however, these moves were still about a decade off.

71. I am referring here mainly to the concluding pages in his *The Order of Things*, pp. 384–385. This notion was picked up and reinforced by Derrida in his essay "The Ends of Man," in *Margins of Philosophy*, pp. 109–136.

72. See Foucault, "Afterword: The Subject and Power," in Hubert L. Dreyfus and Paul Rabinow, *Michel Foucault: Beyond Structuralism and Hermeneutics* (Chicago: University of Chicago Press, 1982), pp. 208–226.

73. Taylor's critique was voiced especially in his *The Ethics of Authenticity* (Cambridge, MA: Harvard University Press, 1992), pp. 55–69. In a central passage there (p. 60), he notes a movement "towards a kind of nihilism, a negation of all horizons of significance. . . . The major figure here is Nietzsche. . . . Aspects of this line of thinking found expression in some strands of modernism, and its has emerged among writers who are often referred to today as postmodern, such as Jacques Derrida or the later Michel Foucault." Regarding Habermas see his *The Philosophical Discourse of Modernity, Twelve Lectures*, trans. Frederick Lawrence (Cambridge, MA: MIT Press, 1987); for my critical response see below, note 95. As I might add, I have always stayed much closer to the thinking of Adorno than Habermas seemed willing to accept; see, e.g., my "Adorno and Heidegger," *Diacritics*, vol. 19 (1989), pp. 82–100; and "Adorno and Heidegger on Modernity," in Iain MacDonald and Krzysztof Ziarek, eds., *Adorno and Heidegger: Philosophical Questions* (Stanford University Press, 2008), pp. 167–181.

74. See Derrida, *The Other Heading: Reflections on Today's Europe*, trans. Pascale-Anne Brault and Michael B. Naas (Bloomington, IN: Indiana University Press, 1992); *Cosmopolites de tous les pays, encore un effort!* (Paris: Galilée, 1997); *Le droit à la philoosphie du point de vue cosmopolitique* (UNESCO: Editions UNESCO, 1997); *On Cosmopolitanism and Forgiveness*, trans. Mark Dooley and Michael Hughes (New York: Routledge, 2001). See also my "Jacques Derrida's Legacy: Democracy to Come," in *The Promise of Democracy: Political*

Agency and Transformation (Albany, NY: State University of New York Press, 2010), pp. 117–134.

75. For a memorial tribute to Foucault see my "Foucault *in memoriam* (1926–1984)," *Human Studies*, vol. 10 (1987), pp. 2–9. See also Edward W. Said, *Orientalism* (New York: Vintage Books, 1979); and my *Beyond Orientalism: Essays on Cross-Cultural Encounter* (Albany, NY: State University of New York Press, 1996).

76. For Foucault's use of *"panopticon"* see his "The Eye of Power," in *Power/Knowledge: Selected Interviews and Other Writings 1972–1977*, ed. Colin Gordon, trans. Colin Gordon et al. (New York: Pantheon Books, 1980), pp. 146–165; also *Discipline and Punish: The Birth of the Prison* (New York: Random House, 1978), pp. 195–228. For my critique of Rorty's "neo-pragmatism" (and its departure from John Dewey's legacy) see my "Democratic Action and Experience" in *The Promise of Democracy*, pp. 63–64; and my "Achieving Our World Democratically: A Response to Richard Rorty," in *Achieving Our World: Toward a Global and Plural Democracy* (Lanham, MD: Rowman and Littlefield, 2001), pp. 91–107.

77. See Claude Lefort, *Machiavelli in the Making*, trans. Michael B. Smith (Evanston, IL: Northwestern University Press, 2012); also *Democracy and Political Theory*, trans. David Macey (Minneapolis, MN: University of Minnesota Press, 1988). Compare also Bernard Flynn, *The Philosophy of Claude Lefort: Interpreting the Political* (Evanston, IL: Northwestern University Press, 2005); and my "Democracy Without Banisters: Reading Claude Lefort," in *The Promise of Democracy*, pp. 187–193.

78. See, e.g., Paul Ricoeur, *History and Truth*; trans. Charles A. Kelby (Evanston, IL: Northwestern University Press, 1965); *The Rule of Metaphor*, trans. Robert Czerny (Toronto: University of Toronto Press, 1977); *Time and Narrative*, 3 vols., trans. Kathleen McLaughlin and David Pelauer (Chicago: University of Chicago Press, 1984–1988).

79. See Ricoeur, *Oneself as Another*, trans. Kathleen Blamey (Chicago: University of Chicago Press, 1992), and my "Oneself as Another: Paul Ricoeur's 'Little Ethics'," in my *Achieving Our World*, pp. 171–188; and "Love and Justice: A Memorial Tribute to Paul Ricoeur," in *In Search of the Good Life: A Pedagogy for Troubled Times* (Lexington: KY: University of Kentucky Press, 2007), pp. 220–235.

80. The lectures were presented at Loyola University in spring of 1981. They were published in revised form as *Language and Politics: Why Does Language Matter to Political Philosophy?* (Notre Dame, IN: University of Notre Dame Press, 1984).

81. The meeting happened in an elevator in the main library building. Noticing a stack of books under my arms, Father Hesburgh asked what I was teaching. When I responded "A seminar on Nietzsche," he simply said: "Good; we are a university." I enjoyed his support throughout his tenure as university president. Unfortunately, after his retirement (in 1987), his Erasmian open-mindedness was not always preserved.

82. See Stephen K. White, ed., *Life-world and Politics: Between Modernity and Postmodernity; Essays in Honor of Fred R. Dallmayr* (Notre Dame, IN: University of Notre Dame Press, 1989); for my Hegel book see note 95 below; see also Iris Marion Young, *Justice and the Politics of Difference* (Princeton: NJ: Princeton University Press, 1990). Young subsequently published some important works on feminist theory; see, e.g., *On Female Body Experience* (New York: Oxford University Press, 2005). Sadly, she died relatively young in 2006. A few years earlier, my first doctoral student at Notre Dame University, Stephen F. Schneck, published another edited volume on my writings; see Schneck, ed., *Letting Be: Fred Dallmayr's Cosmopolitical Vision* (Notre Dame, IN: University of Notre Dame Press, 2006).

83. See Fred Dallmayr and Thomas A. McCarthy, eds., *Understanding and Human Inquiry* (Notre Dame, IN: University of Notre Dame Press, 1977); Seyla Benhabib and Fred Dallmayr, eds., *The Communicative Ethics Controversy* (Cambridge, MA: MIT Press, 1990). For some pieces on my former Purdue colleagues see "Transversal Encounters: Calvin Schrag and Postmodernism," in *Achieving Our World*, pp. 111–128; and "The Relevance of Revelance: Comments on McBride," *Philosophy in Context*, vol. 13 (1983), pp. 71–75.

84. See, e.g., my "Border Crossings: Bernhard Waldenfels on Dialogue," in *Achieving Our World*, pp. 129–146; "On Bernhard Waldenfels," *Social Research*, vol. 56 (1989), pp. 681–712; and my Foreword to his *Order in the Twilight*, trans. David J. Parent (Athens, OH: Ohio University Press, 1996), pp. 167–168. Regarding Richard Bernstein see my "Pragmatics and

Hermeneutics: Bernstein," in *Critical Encounters Between Philosophy and Politics* (Notre Dame, IN: University of Notre Press, 1987), pp. 165–182.

85. See e.g., Richard Ashcraft, *Locke's Two Treatises of Government* (London: Allen & Unwin, 1987); Ashcraft, ed., *John Locke: Critical Assessments* (New York: Routledge, 1991); Kenneth Minogue and Anthony de Crespigny, eds., *Contemporary Political Philosophies* (New York: Dodd, Mead, 1975). Ashcraft passed away too soon in 1995; Minogue in 2013.

86. See Vrajendra Raj Mehta, *A Theory of Politics* (Delhi: Sultan Chand, 1968); Mehta and Thomas Panthan, *Political Ideas in Modern India* (London: Sage Publications, 2006); Ashis Nandy, *The Intimate Enemy* (Delhi: Oxford University Press, 1983); Nandy and D. L. Sheth, eds., *The Multiverse of Democracy* (New Delhi: Sage, 1996); Partha Chatterjee, *The Nation and Its Fragments* (Princeton, NJ: Princeton University Press, 1993); *A Possible India* (New York: Oxford University Press, 1997).

87. Together with an Indian colleague and friend, G. N. Devy, I edited at the time a volume depicting the complex fabric of India's intellectual currents: *Between Tradition and Modernity: India's Search for Identity* (Walnut Creek: Altamira Press, 1998).

88. See, e.g., Bradley J. Makowski, ed., *New Perspectives on Advaita Vedanta: Essays in Commemoration of Richard De Smet* (Leiden: Brill, 2000); Francis X. D'Sa, *Hermeneutics of Encounter* (Vienna: Collection De Nobile, 1994); D'Sa and Elmar Klinger, eds., *Gerechtigkeit im Dialog der Kulturen* (Würzburg: Echter, 2006); John Vattanky, *Gangesa's Philosophy of God* (Madias: Adyar Library, 1984); *A System of Indian Logic* (London: Routledge/Curzon, 2003).

89. See, e.g., Wilhelm Halbfass, *India and Europe: An Essay in Understanding* (Albany: NY: State University of New York Press, 1988); *Tradition and Reflection: Explorations in Indian Thought* (Albany, NY: State University of New York Press, 1991); also my "Exit from Orientalism: Comments on Halbfass," in *Beyond Orientalism*, pp. 115–134.

90. Among the modes of Hindu religiosity, I became particularly fond of Vaishnavism, mainly because of the role of Lord Krishna in the *Bhagavad Gita*. Regarding Jainism, I might add that there are many famous Jain temples in Gujarat, some of them located on hills or mountain tops, like Politana or Mount Girnar (which I visited with some Indian students and friends).

91. See, e.g., Jarava Lal Mehta, *The Philosophy of Martin Heidegger* (New York: Harper & Row, 1971); *India and the West* (Chico, CA: Scholars Press, 1985); *Philosophy and Religion: Essays in Interpretation* (New Delhi: Indian Council of Philosophical Research, 1990); William J. Jackson, ed., *J. L. Mehta on Heidegger, Hermeneutic, and Indian Tradition* (Leiden: Brill, 1992); also my "Heidegger, Bhakti, and Vedanta: A Tribute to J. L. Mehta," in *Beyond Orientalism*, pp. 89–114.

92. To mention some other tours: I frequently visited Delhi and from there took trips to the Taj Mahal and Fatehpur Sikri. At one time, V. R. Mehta (who then was teaching at Jodhpur in Rajasthan) arranged for me to take a trip to Jazelmere, a fabulous old town located in the desert near the border of Pakistan.

93. See *Critical Encounters: Between Philosophy and Politics* (Notre Dame, IN: University of Notre Dame Press, 1987). Alasdair MacIntyre was for many years my colleague in the Department of Philosophy at Notre Dame. I always appreciated his (neo-) Aristotelian emphasis on the practice of "virtues" and also his writing on narrative. The chapter in *Critical Encounters*, titled "Virtue and Tradition: Macintyre," reflects this appreciation, but also signals a crucial difference when it replaces his formula "Nietzsche *or* Aristotle" with the motto "Nietzsche *and* Aristotle." Regarding Michael Theunissen, I was strongly influenced by his book *The Other: Studies in the Social Ontology of Husserl, Heidegger, Sartre, and Buber*, trans. Christopher Macann (Cambridge, MA: MIT Press, 1984). The chapter in *Critical Encounters*, "Dialogue & Otherness: Theunissen," acknowledges this influence, but also critiques as mistaken his "subjectivist" construal of Heidegger's co-being *(Mitsein)*.

94. *Margins of Political Discourse* (Albany, NY: State University of New York Press, 1989). See especially Chapter 2, "Gandhi as Mediator Between East and West," pp. 22–38. Chapter 6, "Hegemony and Democracy," contains my first critical encounter with the work of Laclau and Mouffe. While appreciating the (Foucauldian) stress on political conflict or "antagonism," the Chapter moderates the antimony of conflict by ethical relationality (or a post-

Hegelian *Sittlichkeit*). Compare also my "The Return of the Political: On Chantal Mouffe," *Constellations*, vol. 3 (1996), pp. 115–120.

95. For my critical assessment of *The Philosophical Discourse* see Chapter 3, "The Discourse and Counter-Discourse of Modernity," in *Margins of Philosophy*, pp. 39–72. As I stated there a bit harshly (p. 71): "With a stern and commanding gesture, Nietzsche and his heirs are exiled or banished from the province of reason—a province seemingly entrusted to Habermas's custody. This banishment, however, exacts a price. With his exclusionary policy Habermas inadvertently lends credence to the claim of some Nietzscheans (especially Foucault) that every discourse, including rational discourse, harbors a principle of exclusion." See also my "The Discourse of Modernity: Hegel, Nietzsche, Heidegger (and Habermas)," in *Praxis International*, vol. 8 (1989), pp. 377–406; and "Habermas and Rationality," *Political Theory*, vol. 17 (1988), pp. 553–579.

96. *Between Freiburg and Frankfurt: Toward a Critical Ontology* (see above, note 58). The book contains, among others, chapters on "Adorno and Heidegger," "Heidegger and Marxism," and "Heidegger and Psychotherapy" (with a focus on the so-called "Zollikon Seminars").

97. See *G. W. F. Hegel: Modernity and Politics* (Newbury Park, CA: Sage Publications, 1993; vol. 3 in the series "Modernity and Political Thought"). A new edition of the book was published by Rowman & Littlefield in 2002. As readers will discover, the famous Hegelian "dialectic" plays only a minor or subordinate part in this study. Moreover, partly under the influence of Adorno's "negative dialectics," I tend to bracket the Hegelian notion of a final synthesis.

98. See *The Other Heidegger* (Ithaca, NY: Cornell University Press, 1993); also my "Rethinking the Political: Some Heideggerian Contributions," *Review of Politics*, vol. 52 (1990), pp. 524–552; and "The Underside of Modernity: Adorno, Heidegger, and Dussel," *Constellations*, vol. 11 (2004), pp. 102–120. As one should note, *The Other Heidegger* was composed at a time when some of his major texts of the 1930's were not yet available. Their subsequent publication convinced me that the fabled "*Kehre*" was not only a metaphysical turning but a profound turning-away from the horrors of the Nazi regime.

99. On Waldenfels see note 84 above.

100. On Bernstein see my "Pragmatism and Hermeneutics: Bernstein," in *Critical Encounters*, pp. 165–182. In my view, Bernstein corrected some of the mistaken accents of Richard Rorty's work. Although presenting himself as Dewey's direct heir, Rorty's credentials were for me always in doubt. All the troubling polarities of modern Western thought—subject/object, self/other, private/public—which Dewey (in good Hegelian fashion) had tried to overcome, seemed to be revived in Rorty's writings. I also found unhelpful the dichotomy between "science" and "edification" proposed in his *Philosophy and the Mirror of Nature* (Princeton, NY: Princeton University Press, 1979).

101. Reiner Schürmann, *Heidegger on Being and Acting: From Principles to Anarchy* (Bloomington, IN: Indiana University Press, 1987); Schürmann passed away in 1993. Regarding Heller see, e.g., her *An Ethics of Personality* (Oxford, UK: Blackwell, 1996).

102. See my "Opening the Doors of Interpretation: In Memory of Nasr Abu Zayd and Muhammed al-Jabri," in *Being in the World: Dialogue and Cosmopolis* (Lexington, KY: University of Kentucky Press, 2013), pp. 177–194. I might also add here that, as a member of the International Advisory Board of the NGO "RESET" (headquartered in Rome), I participated several times in the so-called "Istanbul Seminars" organized by that group.

103. See, e.g., Eliot Deutsch, *Advaita Vedanta: A Philosophical Reconstruction* (Honolulu, HI: East-West Center Press, 1969); Deutsch, ed., *Culture and Modernity: East-West Philosophical Perspectives* (Honolulu, HI: University of Hawaii Press, 1991); Gerald J. Larson, *India's Agony over Religion* (Albany, NY: State University of New York Press, 1995); Raimon Panikkar, *Myth, Faith, and Hermeneutics: Cross-Cultural Studies* (New York: Paulist Press, 1973); Tu Weiming, *Confucian Thought: Selfhood as Creative Transformation* (Albany, NY: State University of New York Press, 1985); Roger T. Ames and David L. Hall, *Thinking through Confucius* (Albany, NY: State University of New York Press, 1987); Henry Rosemont Jr., *The Chinese Mirror* (LaSalle, IL: Open Court, 1991); Marietta Stepaniants and Ron Bontekoe, eds., *Justice and Democracy: Cross-Cultural Perspectives* (Honolulu, HI: University of Hawaii Press, 1997). Compare also my "Western Thought and Indian Thought" and "*Sunyata*

East and West" in *Beyond Orientalism*, pp. 135–148, 175–199; "Humanity and Humanization: Comments on Confucianism," in *Alternative Visions*, pp. 123–144; and "The Natural Theology of the Chinese: Leibniz and Confucianism" (on Rosemont), *In Search of the Good Life*, pp. 80–94.

104. See, e.g., Douglas Allen, *Culture and Self: Philosophical and Religious Perspectives, East and West* (Boulder, Colo.: Westview Press, 1997); Joseph Prabhu, *The Intercultural Challenge of Raimon Panikkar* (Maryknoll, NY: Orbis Books, 1996); Michiko Yusa, *Zen and Philosophy: An Intellectual Biography of Nishida Kitaro* (Honolulu, HI: University of Hawaii Press, 2002).

105. Keiji Nishitani, *Religion and Nothingness*, trans. Jan Van Bragt (Berkeley, CA: University of California Press, 1982).

106. See my "Heidegger and Zen Buddhism: A Salute to Keiji Nishitani," in *The Other Heidegger*, pp. 200–226.

107. See note 103 above.

108. See "Non-Western Political Thought," Special Issue of *The Review of Politics*, vol. 59 (1997), pp. 421–647; Dallmayr, ed., *Border Crossings: Toward a Comparative Political Theory* (Lanham, MD: Rowman & Littlefield/Lexington Books, 1999).

109. See my "Beyond Monologue: For a Comparative Political Theory," *Perspectives on Politics*, vol. 2 (2004), pp. 249–257.

110. For me, the latter agenda was particularly upsetting because it threatened the Erasmian balance of "*fides et eruditio*," by reducing free inquiry tendentially to a handmaiden of dogmatic faith.

111. See *Alternative Visions: Paths in the Global Village* (Lanham, MD: Rowman & Littlefield, 1998).

112. See, e.g., Chandra Muzaffar, *Global Ethic or Global Hegemony?* (London: Asean Academic Press, 2005); *Muslims, Dialogue, Terror* (Selangor: Just World Trust, 2003); *Rights, Religion and Reform* (London: Routledge Carzon, 2002); Paul Knitter and Muzaffar, eds., *Subverting Greed: Religious Perspectives on the Global Economy* (Maryknoll, NY: Orbis Books, 2002).

113. *Achieving Our World: Toward a Global and Plural Democracy* (Rowman & Littlefield, 2001).

114. *Dialogue Among Civilization: Some Exemplary Voices* (Palgrave/St. Martin's Press, 2002).

115. *Peace Talks—Who Will Listen?* (Notre Dame, IN: University of Notre Dame Press, 2004). Compare also my "Gandhi and Islam: A Heart-and-Mind Unity?" in V.R. Mehta and Thomas Pantham, eds., *Political Ideas in Modern India: Thematic Explorations* (New Delhi: Sage, 2006), pp. 206–220.

116. *Small Wonder: Global Power and Its Discontents* (Lanham, MD: Lexington Books, 2005). See also my "But on a Quiet Day . . . A Tribute to Arundhati Roy," in Sura P. Rath et al., eds., *Reflections on Literature, Criticism and Theory* (Delhi: Pencraft International, 2004), pp. 231–247.

117. I paid tribute to Daya Krishna, and also to philosopher Ramchandra Gandhi (a grandson of the Mahatma) who both passed away in 2007 later in my "Reason and Lifeworld: Two Exemplary Indian Thinkers," in *Integral Pluralism: Beyond Culture Wars* (Lexington, KY: University Press of Kentucky, 2010), pp. 143–165. My book *Dialogue Among Civilizations* (2002) was dedicated to Gadamer; the content of the entire book, in fact, is a tribute to, and saturated by, the teachings of Gadamer. Compare also my "The Enigma of Health: Hans-Georg Gadamer at 100," *The Review of Politics*, vol. 62 (2000), pp. 327–350; and my "Dialogue of Civilizations: A Gadamerian Perspective," *Global Dialogue*, vol. 3 (2001), pp. 64–75.

118. Some theological studies I undertook at the time encouraged me in this belief. Most important to me was the reading of some of the writings of Nikolaus Cusanus. Other texts important to me were Richard Kearney, *The God Who May Be: A Hermeneutics of Religion* (Bloomington, IN: Indiana University Press, 2001); and John D. Caputo, *The Weakness of God: A Theology of the Event* (Bloomington, IN: Indiana University Press, 2006).

119. Alasdair MacIntyre, *After Virtue: A Study in Moral Theory*, 3rd ed. (Notre Dame, IN: University of Notre Dame Press, 2007).

120. Compare, e.g., Roger Crisp and Michael Slote, ed., *Virtue Ethics* (New York: Oxford University Press, 1997); Charles E. Curran and Lisa A. Fullam, eds., *Virtue* (Mahwah, NJ: Paulist Press, 2011); and Daniel C. Russell, eds., *The Cambridge Companion to Virtue Ethics* (New York: Cambridge University Press, 2013).

121. Dallmayr, *In Search of the Good Life: A Pedagogy for Troubled Times* (Lexington, NY: University Press of Kentucky, 2007).

122. *The Promise of Democracy: Political Agency and Transformation* (Albany, NY: State University of New York, 2010). See also my "Jacques Derrida's Legacy: Democracy to Come," in Kailash C. Baral and R. Radhakinhnan, eds., *Theory after Derrida* (New Delhi: Taylor & Francis India, 2009), pp. 24–26.

123. See *Integral Pluralism: Beyond Culture Wars* (cited in note 117).

124. See especially William James, *A Pluralistic Universe* (1909; reprint, New York: Longmans, Green, 1932); William E. Connolly, *The Ethos of Pluralization* (Minneapolis, MN: University of Minnesota Press, 1995); also Charles Taylor, *The Ethics of Authenticity* (Cambridge, MA: Harvard University Press, 1991); *A Catholic Modernity*, ed. James L. Heft (New York: Oxford University Press, 1999).

125. See my *Comparative Political Theory: An Introduction* (New York: Palgrave Macmillan, 2010).

126. See, e.g., Thomas Berry, *Evening Thoughts: Reflections on the Earth as Sacred Community* (Berkeley, CA: University of California Press, 2006); *The Sacred Universe* (New York: Columbia University Press, 2009); Raimon Panikkar, *The Cosmotheandric Experience* (Maryknoll, NY: Orbis Books, 1993).

127. See *Return to Nature? An Ecological Counter-History* (Lexington, KY: University Press of Kentucky, 2011).

128. Hannah Arendt, "On Violence," in *Crises of the Republic* (New York: Harcourt Brace Jovanovich, 1969), p. 177. Compare also my "Radical Changes in the Muslim World: Whither Democracy?" in *Being in the World: Dialogue and Cosmopolis* (Lexington: University Press of Kentucky, 2013), pp. 162–176.

129. In the opening decade of this century I was able to pay several visits to Iran, presenting lectures in Tehran and at a seminary in Qom, while also enjoying the sights in Isfahan and Shiraz (especially the tombs of Hafiz and Sadi). What particularly struck me during my visits was the intellectual vibrancy among faculty, students, and ordinary people—a vibrancy somewhat at odds with the cumbersome or lopsided political structure of the country. Regarding that structure, see my "Religion, Democracy, and Iran: A Modest Proposal," *Comparative Studies of South Asia, Africa, and the Middle East* 27 (2007): 503–508; see also my "Religion, Politics, and Islam: Toward Multiple Modes of Democracy," in *The Promise of Democracy*, pp. 155–167. As I might add, I have served as "external examiner" for several Iranian doctoral candidates (some of them expatriates), including Nader Hashemi, Hossein Mesbahian, Ali Mesbah, and Siavash Saffari. Several of my books have been translated into Farsi.

130. The Forum regularly assembled prominent experts and practitioners in different fields, including lawyers, economists, academics, religious leaders, and media people. As an NGO, the Forum did not seek to duplicate or interfere with the work of governments; rather, it acted as a kind of public conscience reminding governments and policy makers of their ethical duties in this world. By comparison with my membership in SPEP, SACP, and other societies, participation in the Forum added the dimension of practical engagement in deliberations about concrete global affairs. See in this context my "Who Are We? What Is World Public Forum—Dialogue of Civilizations?" in Dallmayr and Vladimir Yakunin, eds., *Some Global Rays of Hope* (Moscow: World Public Forum, 2012), pp. 20–26.

131. See, e.g., Daniel A. Bell, *Beyond Liberal Democracy: Political Thinking for an East Asian Context* (Princeton, NJ: Princeton University Press, 2006); and my "Exiting Liberal Democracy? Bell and Confucian Thought," in *The Promise of Democracy*, pp. 169–185.

132. See Dallmayr and Zhao Tingyang, eds., *Contemporary Chinese Political Thought: Debates and Perspectives* (Lexington: University Press of Kentucky, 2012).

133. One of my early doctoral students in America, Hongwoo Kim, on his return to Korea became professor at Seoul National University. After his retirement there he became associated

with Kyung Hee University. One of his students, Chung-Shig Shin, translated my book *The Other Heidegger* into Korean.

134. Compare Martha Nussbaum, *Not for Profit* (Princeton, NJ: Princeton University Press, 2010); Nussbaum, *Cultivating Humanity* (Cambridge, MA: Harvard University Press, 1997); and Elise Boulding, *Building a Global Civil Culture* (Syracuse, NY: Syracuse University Press, 1990).

135. See *Being in the World: Dialogue and Cosmopolis* (Lexington: University Press of Kentucky, 2013).

136. See especially *"Herkunft aber bleibt stets Zukunft": Martin Heidegger und die Gottes-frage*, ed. Paola-Ludovica Coriando (Frankfurt: Klostermann, 1998). Compare also Alexander Stille, *The Future of the Past* (New York: Farrar, Strauss & Giroux, 2002).

137. See Arendt, *Between Past and Future: Six Exercises in Political Thought* (Cleveland, OH: Meridian Books, 1963).

138. In the society, which I joined late in my life (the World Public Forum), there was a practice among Russian participants to travel on Easter to Jerusalem to bring the Easter light, in the form of a big candle, to Moscow where it serves to light up a small ocean of candles in the central cathedral. I think this practice is a good metaphor for our lives where we receive inspiration from somewhere far off—not to hoard it possessively but to pass it on to the people we encounter on our journey.

Appendix A

"Sehnsucht Dorthin":
A Response to Rasmussen and Flynn

I want to thank my friends David Rasmussen and Bernard Flynn for their thoughtful comments, for having undertaken the trouble of reading my book *In Search of the Good Life.*[1] I feel honored by their attentiveness and critical reflections. Pondering such comments always involves a learning experience: one learns not only about the views of others but also about one's own thought and how it may be expressed, adequately or inadequately, in a given text. So, responding is rewarding; but it is also—especially in this case—difficult. Responding to Rasmussen and Flynn I feel like I am responding, or expected to respond, in a way to John Rawls and Hannah Arendt, or more broadly to (what is called) "political liberalism" and "civic republicanism" respectively. In David's case, there are, in addition to Rawls, occasional friendly gestures also toward Hegel, Charles Taylor and others; in Bernie's case, Arendtian references are amplified by appeals to Machiavelli and Claude Lefort. Still, unless I am very much mistaken, behind these complexities there looms this basic issue: How does the quest for the "good life" relate to political liberalism and/or civic republicanism? To answer this question quickly and in summary fashion, let me say that—despite certain affinities—it relates to them in the mode of a challenge or contestation.

I turn first to David's comments, mainly because of the greater prominence (I believe) of political liberalism in the modern Western, especially American, tradition. Some preliminary remarks. David starts out by noting correctly that I take my initial point of departure from ordinary human conduct, from the conduct of *homines idiotae*, that is, from the "life-world" (and not from the Cartesian *cogito* or pure reason). He also notes that I distance myself—or rather: that the ordinary life-world distances itself—from the "liberal disaggregation of social life" which "privatizes" moral or ethical conduct. He adds that, in my view, it is mainly "liberalism that in some sense got us to this unhappy place." (I would say: "a certain kind of liberalism," namely, late-modern Western liberalism—but let it stand for the time being.) In an accommodating vein, David agrees about "the current malaise with the shock of our having found ourselves in this unwanted and uncalled for war and the public culture [i.e., the culture of violence] that brought it to us": Somewhat later he notes that what I challenge is probably "neo-liberalism with the 'Washington Consensus' as the basis for its somewhat ideological approach to democracy." He even adds that "the neo-liberal paradigm— which is [or was] at the heart of the Bush administration and which conforms very nicely with that same administration's neo-conservative policy—is to be admonished." (Here just a brief aside. "Admonished"? After having thrown the entire world into economic chaos through reckless greed and irresponsibility, does neo-liberalism simply need to be admonished? And regarding foreign policy, I recall that, over sixty years ago, leaders of a nation unleashing "uncalled-for wars" against other countries were not admonished but tried and convicted by an international tribunal.)

Let me not digress. David's basic point is that, while the neo-liberal paradigm needs to be rebuked, "one need not lay this critique at the feet of political liberalism." A bit earlier he states: "I disagree that it is liberalism, that is, liberalism in its best form as political liberalism, which brought us to this point. Liberalism in its best form has toleration as its principle of justice. . . My position . . . is supported on the basis of an informed political liberalism." The phrase "political liberalism" here obviously stems from John Rawls. But, as previously indicated, David is not a narrow-minded Rawlsian, but is willing here and there to assimilate a dose of Hegelian and Taylorian teachings. In his words, the problem with my approach—which is a cross-cultural approach—is "that the very principle which makes possible the relationship with other cultures is the principle of toleration, a liberal principle. And beyond that there is a certain strategy which can be endorsed for the 'recognition' of other cultures as cultures and political systems, which have their own claims of legitimacy." Now recognition (*Anerkennung*) is, of course, a term dear to Hegel, Taylor, and more recently Paul Ricoeur and Axel Honneth. David also endorses the notion of an "overlapping consensus," a term employed, for different reasons, by both Rawls and Taylor (although Taylor is surely not a Rawlsian).

Just a brief comment here on the claim that "toleration" is a "liberal principle." I would grant that toleration is liberal in the sense of the classical virtue of "liberality" or generosity; but I would not grant that it is liberal in the sense of modern Western liberalism as inaugurated by Hobbes and Locke (and continued by Rawls and others). In his comments on my book, David makes reference to what I call there "Prominent Searchers in the Past." The first among them is St. Bonaventure. It so happens that he was a leader of the so-called "conventional" (or liberal) wing of the Franciscan order, as opposed to the more restrictive or austere wing. But he was surely not a Lockean liberal greatly concerned with individual privileges and private property. Nicolaus of Cusa is mentioned by David as one who was able "to appreciate Muslim culture even after the fall of Constantinople." Again: no Lockean or Rawlsian liberal. And Leibniz who was very critical of Descartes (and by implication of Locke) celebrated the "Natural Theology of the Chinese" against orthodox church doctrines. If David had browsed a bit further through my book, he would have found an Appendix titled "Building Peace—How?" There I pay tribute to the Iranian philosopher Abdulkarim Soroush who, in late 2004, was awarded the Erasmus Prize in Amsterdam, a prize given in memory of the great Dutch humanist and peace-maker. On the occasion of this award, Soroush appropriately delivered a talk titled "Treatise on Tolerance," invoking in support of his theme not Locke or Mill but chiefly the great Sufi poets and thinkers Rumi and Hafiz. (Perhaps I might add that my earlier book *Peace Talks—Who Will Listen?* was in large measure inspired by Erasmus, seen as a great non-Lockean liberal.) I return to the issue of tolerance a bit later.

At this point I want to address the issue of "political liberalism" more directly. I wish to make three points: first, regarding the linkage between liberalism and neo-liberalism; secondly, regarding one of the founders of modern liberalism who is often and conveniently forgotten; and lastly, regarding the adequacy or inadequacy of liberal tolerance. On the first point: the connection between modern liberalism and neo-liberalism (in my view) is not accidental or fortuitous. According to common agreement, modern liberalism had its main roots in the Glorious Revolution, the Bill of Rights (of 1689), and the work of John Locke. Thus, it arose when the traditional ethical fabric of society was still largely intact. Into this fabric, Locke inserted his basic liberal principle: that everyone is endowed with the right to life, liberty, and property (or estate). "Everyone" here means every individual. Thus, surreptitiously, the linchpin of Cartesian philosophy, the autonomous ego, was inserted into society, with potentially "disaggregating" effects. But as I said, disaggregation was at the time still cushioned by traditional mores and, above all, by the context of an agrarian society. Locke stipulated that one can accumulate only that much property as would not spoil; but he already made allowance for a larger accumulation of goods which cannot spoil: money or capital. This concession became crucial with the change from an agrarian to an industrial society, a change which gave increasing prominence to the economic market while pushing both politics and ethics to the margins. During the 19th century, the key motto of liberalism became: "the government (or regime) which governs least governs best" (that is, is best able to protect private property). But this was only the onset of the real upsurge of capitalism in the later 19th and 20th centuries when industrial capitalism was steadily overtaken by finance capitalism. By that time, all the cushions or buffers of the past have been stripped away, leaving behind only the bare-knuckles profit motive or what Richard Falk calls "predatory capitalism." What this entails we experience today. In any case, the road leading from Lockean liberalism to neo-liberalism is not simply an aberration.

Let me get to my second point—and this is also something we experience today. Next to Locke, there is another ancestor to modern liberalism, his darker double or twin: Thomas Hobbes. For Hobbes, human or civil rights are of little or no value unless backed up by sovereign power. A key sentence is that "words without the sword" are empty utterances, unable to provide safety or security to anyone. Hobbes transferred the fear of violent death that grips individuals in the "state of nature" to the civil state where it becomes fear of sovereign power. His work radically and disdainfully brushed aside the Aristotelian legacy of politics and ethics, and thus the cushion on which Locke still relied. For Hobbes, individuals are not naturally social or political creatures, and the political regime is *not* a natural regime; rather, the modern state is a construct, an artifact, an "artificial body." (Here, David seems to be quite wrong when he says that the modern state is a natural entity.) For Hobbes, that state arises from a "social contract," an act of civil engineering. But, as I said, a contract is only a string of words unless backed up by sovereign might. Locke retained the social contract, but concealed the fear factor. Rawls' "original position" likewise is a kind of social contract; but again the fear factor is hidden. Yet, that factor cannot be hidden for long. Every time when there is trouble in modern Western society, the fear factor leaps into the foreground. After September 11, liberalism in America turned into a liberalism of fear, that is, a Hobbesian liberalism. But the upsurge of Hobbes is inevitable. The more the cushion of social and political ethics is stripped away, the more the bonds of mutual sympathy are obliterated, the more necessary becomes the resort to power and fear. And under "fear's empire"—to borrow the phrase of Benjamin Barber—the niceties of Lockean liberalism go by the wayside.

My third point concerning tolerance is closely linked with the preceding discussion. As sponsored by Rasmussen and many others, liberal tolerance does not seem fully adequate. In the absence of a frame of goodness (or a frame of ethical significance), how far does tolerance extend? Does it also extend to racists, torturers, rapists, Abu Ghraib? Of course, the liberal does not wish to tolerate such horrors. But all the liberal can say is: these practices are not tolerable because they are against the "law." Yet, what if the rapist retorts: why should I obey the law? Since the liberal cannot respond "because the law is good," all he or she can say is: "It is the law and if you do not obey, we shall force you to obey. We have punishments." Thus, the Hobbesian fear factor is the liberal's last resort. To put the issue a bit differently: tolerance cannot simply be equivalent to neutral indifference. Here we enter a difficult terrain. As we know, the modern liberal state is claimed to be "neutral" vis-à-vis all ethical and religious beliefs because they are said to be purely "private" and insofar irrelevant. However, ethical and religious beliefs are liable to be reflected in conduct and, to this extent, have practical effects. At this point, the criterion of judgment can no longer be "private" irrelevance but has to involve substantive considerations. As it seems to me, public tolerance of diverse beliefs and practices is predicated not so much on their ethical indifference but rather on the assumption of ethical significance: the assumption that, no matter how alien, beliefs and practices remain ethically redeemable by being ultimately—perhaps obliquely—oriented toward the common good.

It is this concern with ethical significance and ethical mutuality which is at the heart of Hegel's concept of "recognition." It is primarily through this concept that Hegel sought to tame and overcome the inherent rapaciousness of modern individual self-interest and lust for power and possessions. Here, no doubt, we are face to face with the imposing grandeur of Hegelian philosophy (of what one may call Hegel's "ethical liberalism"). Still, today, we may wish to go even beyond the concept of recognition to the extent that the latter is a form of "cognition" or knowledge (harking back to the Cartesian *cogito*). Perhaps what is needed today, above and beyond recognition in the sense of "knowing-with", is a "being-with" in the sense of Heideggerian *Mitsein*. "Being-with" here means sharing a world together, with its joys and sorrows, a sharing animated not only by cognition but by passion and compassion. In his important book *Critique and Disclosure*, Nikolas Kompridis states the issue well when he writes (p. 210) that "the act of recognizing the other will also involve a struggle with oneself, a struggle in which one's own self-understanding . . . will be at stake. That is why such a struggle is at once cognitive and affective, demanding an examination of one's reasons and one's sensibility, and of each in the light of the other." And Heidegger's student Hans-Georg Gadamer ably pinpointed the gist of "being-with" by stating: "The highest and most elevated aim we can strive for . . . is to partake in the other, to share the other's alterity. [In this way] we may learn to experience human others as the 'other of ourselves' in order to partake in one another."

There are many other points in Rasmussen's comments which would deserve a response but which I have to bypass. Let me just briefly lift up two issues. One concerns Schiller whom David professes to cherish. In my reading, Schiller did not merely follow or "reconstruct" Kant's philosophy, but tried to mediate between the "moral sense" tradition (from Shaftsbury and Hutcheson to Hume) and Kantian deonotology, and then move beyond both toward the aesthetic "play drive" (which earned him Hegel's applause). The other concerns the "good life." David acknowledges that I do not advance *one* theory of the good life, in fact that I do not advance *any* "theory" of it. Yet, he remains critical of any notion of the "good" or "good life." Behind this attitude, of course, there is the concern for individual freedom and the refusal to submit to any doctrinaire authority—a concern and a refusal I actually share and appreciate. However, goodness for me is not a doctrine or a proposition but a frame or horizon of significance—a frame without which Kantian morality and also David's "deontology" would not get off the ground. (As we know, this issue has been widely discussed under the auspices of the respective primacy of the "right" and the "good"—and for me, Taylor's arguments regarding the precedence of the latter are persuasive.)

Like David, Bernard Flynn credits me with not presenting a full fledged doctrine of ethics or the good life. As he sees it, my book offers a number of "examples" or possible guideposts; with Stanley Cavell one might speak here of "possible lives" or alternative possibilities of life. In fact, I deliberately designed the first part of the book as a kind of picture gallery of different lives coming from different backgrounds and traditions—lives which display some kind of goodness or, as Bernie says, "something like a lived social ethic." None of the lives are quite the same. They do *not* illustrate a uniform model, and I certainly do not attribute to them an "exemplary causality" (in the Kantian sense). Nobody could follow precisely any of these examples, and certainly not all of them together. So, my starting point is phenomenological: the buzzing diversity of the "life-world." For phenomenological I might also say "ethnomethodological." I do not begin by rigidly pitting scientific medicine against folk medicine nor systematic (epistemic) knowledge against insight or experiential wisdom. My assumption is that, in pursuing their questions, philosophers not only gain knowledge but also undergo a kind of seasoning, a transformative experience which enables them to live their lives differently: soberly or wisely not rashly, thoughtfully not thoughtlessly, "reckfully" not recklessly. Wisdom here is "*sophia*" not "*episteme*," and it counts among the Aristotelian virtues.

The main gist of Bernie's comments is his endorsement of "civic republicanism" (as over against a procedural political liberalism). I am actually more favorable to civic republicanism than to political liberalism. The Introduction of my book pays tribute at length to Walter Lippmann, a civic republican well known for his books *The Good Society* and *Public Philosophy*. There are similarities as well as differences between David's liberalism and Bernie's republicanism. One similarity resides in a certain aversion to metaphysical and/or religious speculation. Another similarity consists in a shared "neutrality" vis-à-vis culture and cultural/religious differences. To this extent, there is perhaps an "overlapping consensus" between the two positions. The main difference derives from the focal point: which in the one case is the individual, in the other case the public regime. Liberalism is primarily concerned with the advantages accruing to individuals, republicanism with the advantages accruing to the republic or the public realm. Another difference derives from the much older pedigree of republicanism compared with modern liberalism. Republicanism can trace its roots back to the Roman and, beyond that, to the Athenian republic. The crucial emphasis of civic republicanism is on citizenship, on how to be a citizen, a *cives*, in a republican regime. Now, obviously, the quality of citizenship depends on the quality of the republic. And thereon hangs a tale. Briefly put: can one be a good citizen in a bad or corrupt republic?

This question was still very much alive in Roman times. Cicero—a learned civic republican—celebrated citizenship in a good or virtuous republic, especially in his books *De republica* and *De officiis*. He drew his inspiration mainly from the Greeks, particularly Plato and Aristotle. Among Greek philosophers, Plato is famous especially for his book titled *The Republic*. As one recalls, Plato there presented the republic as inhabited by a deep tension, a profound struggle or *agon*: the struggle between the "city of pigs" devoted to mere self-satisfaction, and the "other" city devoted to the pursuit of justice and goodness. It is the latter city which Socrates tried to articulate as a "city in speech" (or in creative imagination). The same rift or tension is captured by the so-called "divided line" which separates the shadowy "cave" and its cave-dwellers from the lighted region of truth. For Plato, any move across the dividing line involved a turning-around, a *metanoia* or existential transformation (we might call it a "*Kehre*"). He famously also described philosophizing as a kind of dying. Aristotle built upon Plato. Without rejecting the Platonic *agon*, he merely softened its edges by inserting it into a slow learning process or pedagogy, a steady habituation in the practice of virtues. This slow pedagogy is adequate in normal times, when it is possible (without excessive grief or martyrdom) to be a good citizen in a good republic. But when things go bad, the Platonic edge quickly re-surfaces. By the time of St. Augustine, things had gone terribly wrong; in Rome, Christians were slaughtered to entertain republicans. So, Augustine revived and radicalized the Platonic dividing line by depicting a profound tension (though not antithesis) between the "earthly city" and the "heavenly city." While, in his portrayal, the former city is governed by selfish desire or love of self, the second city is open to a love "beyond," a love going beyond self-satisfaction toward genuine goodness.

From Greece and Rome, civic republicanism has traveled a long distance. Basically, its history can be read as a progressive stream-lining or flattening-out of the Platonic *agon*. Lying dormant during much of the Middle Ages, civic republicanism in the Roman sense was revived by Machiavelli—but with a twist: a pronounced bias against the Middle Ages and a (basically justified) opposition to clerical rule. To a large extent, the classical *agon* was now replaced by an intra-mundane *agon* or struggle: the struggle between factions and between princely and republican regimes (depicted respectively in *The Prince* and the *Discourses*). Significantly, Machiavelli relied for republican inspiration on the historian Livy, rather than on Cicero; as a corollary, the latter's emphasis on civic virtues was replaced by the stress on *virtú*, a kind of manly virility and self-assertiveness animated by the love of glory. The tradition was further streamlined in the French Revolution. In the aftermath of that event, French civic republicanism became radically "laïc," that is, virulently anti-clerical and anti-religious, thus potentially blending into positivism. Progressively, struggle was reduced to the conflict between political parties, social factions and movements, with economic competition in due course overshadowing the public domain. In more recent times, a fresh strong impulse to civic republicanism was provided by Hannah Arendt. By contrast to most liberals, Arendt sought to rescue the "public domain" from the stranglehold of capitalist economics, and the *vita activa* from labor and instrumental work. Despite these innovations, however, her writings (in my view) did not fully restore the classical legacy. Although critical in some respects, she adopted from French republicanism at least the laïcist or anti-religious impulse. More important, however, was her sidelining of Aristotelian ethics and Ciceronian civic virtues in favor of a celebration of *virtú*: the display of individual virtuosity in the public realm.

While David is concerned about the notion of the "good," Bernard Flynn is troubled mainly by references to religious faith. As he writes: "As of late I have given a lot of thought to the emergence of explicitly theological dimensions in political philosophy, both from the right and the left." What troubles him most, I think, is a certain right-wing political theology, associated in recent times chiefly with the work of Carl Schmitt—a theology which, insisting that "all authority comes from God," centerstages "the tradition of obedience to a divinely established authority." Needless to say, I am equally troubled by this conflation of politics and faith. (In this connection, I wish Bernie had given more attention to my chapter on Paul Ricoeur, entitled "Religious Freedom," which contains a sharp critique of the so-called "Christian Right" in America.) But in my view, the same worries can hardly extend to the thought of Benjamin or Levinas, and even less to Latin American "liberation theology" and the "new political theology" (formulated by Jürgen Moltmann and Johann Baptist Metz). I place myself more in the latter camp. Bernie acknowledges that this religious outlook can provide powerful impulses to political movements such as the civil rights movement and the anti-war movement. (I actually believe that it has given *more* boost to these movements than American civic republicanism.) He worries, however, that such impulses cannot be politically embodied or "incarnated." Yet, has the civil rights movement not led to very tangible legal and social changes? And has the anti-war movement not contributed to ending the Vietnam War (and hopefully soon the Iraq War)? What he fails to notice is that the religious impulses I invoke operate first of all on the level of "civil society" (rather than the state), benefiting there from the "free exercise of religion" clause. But in operating on that level, they contribute to the change or transformation of the prevailing "civic culture," thereby affecting the quality of the "city" itself. Here we are back to the question: How can one be a citizen in a bad or corrupt city? Something has to change—and citizenship by itself (mere membership in the city) does not provide sufficient leverage.

But basically, Bernie's worries are misplaced: my book is not a book of religious philosophy or political theology, but of political or "public philosophy" (in Walter Lippmann's sense). Of course, I am willing to define the "public" or "public domain" broadly so as to include religious people as well as secular or non-religious people (I am not sure whether Leibniz, Montesquieu, and Schiller—to whom chapters in my book are devoted—were strictly speaking religious people). In a sense, I appeal both to "religious humanists" and "secular humanists," as long as both are willing to search for the "good life"—which also means a search for the "good city." My own deeper worry is that both political liberalism and civic republicanism have become too complacent and fit too neatly into the prevailing status quo. In a way, they have become theories or doctrines (perhaps dogmas)—which is not quite adequate in "troubled times." In a sense, what I suggest is that the doctrines of political liberalism and civic republicanism need to return to ignorance or "unknowledge"—the unknowledge of a Socrates and Nicolaus of Cusa (*docta ignorantia*)—and start searching again: searching for the key to the city. This is hard; it involves unlearning, a kind of self-deflation. Any genuine ethics, and especially any religious ethics, inevitably requires self-overcoming, self-transformation. Bernie complains that the republican tradition to which he subscribes knows "nothing of either self-abnegation or self-surrender." This attests to the streamlining of that tradition to which I alluded above. Merleau-Ponty knew better; at one point he writes: "What needs to be learned is a dispossession." I believe his friend and student Claude Lefort—to whom Bernie extensively refers—would have agreed. (I do not have space here to outline my somewhat different reading of Lefort.) Surely Gandhi would have agreed. As he said at one point: if you want to be good to others, you have to try to "reduce yourself to zero." Again, this is a pedagogy for hard and troubled times.

Bernie believes that "there is no such thing as authentic Christian citizenship," because a Christian (and probably any genuinely religious person) is "not a citizen." Well, this depends. Clearly, a religious person cannot be a comfortable citizen in a bad or corrupt city. But this does not mean that he/she relinquishes citizenship altogether. The religious person as well as the genuinely ethical person, one might say, express in their conduct not just private wishes but anticipate an "other" city—the city called by Socrates a "city in speech," by Cicero a good republic, by Alfarabi a "virtuous city," while religious believers prefer to call it the "promised land," the land of the "Mahdi," the land of the Maitreya Buddha. In his *Being and Time*, Heidegger states that higher than actuality is potentiality or possibility. My book was written for troubled or wounded people, uncomfortable with actuality. It invites them to search for a possible land, a possible city. And I cast my fishing net widely: to include religious and non-religious people, and among the former Christians, Jews, Muslims, Hindus, Buddhists, Confucians, and many others. My assumption is that they all wish to articulate "goodness" and the "good life" in different, though not radically incompatible ways. For goodness involves a mode of sharing with or being-with.

The character of the search is well captured in the Klee painting which figures on the cover of my book. Bernie somewhat incorrectly states its title as "Mural from the Template of Desires Hither." Actually, it is "temple" not "template." The German title, chosen by Klee, is still more telling: "Wand-bild aus dem Tempel der Sehnsucht Dorthin." The arrows point in several directions (as Bernie says), but they also point upward—or perhaps sideways upward (toward what Merleau-Ponty called "the invisible of the visible"). Most importantly, the key German term is "Sehnsucht" which is not simply any desire—if we mean by desire an impulse of selfish appropriation. Heidegger mentions somewhere that, for Schelling, the divine ground was not a metaphysical substance but rather "Sehnsucht." Beyond simple desire, that term denotes a longing or yearning, and "Sehnsucht Dorthin" a longing thereto, beyond our immediate grasp—a longing which, like love, ultimately points to infinity.

NOTE

1. This paper was published in *Philosophy and Social Criticism* 35 (2009): 1133–1142. It responded to David M. Rasmussen, "Political Liberalism and the Good Life" (1119–1125) and Bernard Flynn, "Review of *In Search of the Good Life*" (1127–1132) in the same volume. Both Rasmussen and Flynn commented on my *In Search of the Good Life: A Pedagogy for Troubled Times* (Lexington: University Press of Kentucky, 2007). See also Nikolas Kompridis, *Critique and Disclosure: Critical Theory Between Past and Future* (Cambridge, MA: MIT Press, 2006).

Appendix B

Reason and Dialogue:
My Road to Intercultural Studies

In retrospect, Marcel Proust writes (I paraphrase), early experiences some-times assume the character of a presage or premonition. In many ways, his words apply to my life's journey. A native of Germany, I grew up in a country marked by its strong philosophical penchant but also by its regional and local diversity. As one should recall, Germany for the longest part of her history was not a unified structure but a sprawling panorama of small king-doms, principalities, duchies, and "free cities"—all held together by the loose and almost mystical umbrella of what was called the "Holy Roman Empire." Resisting rigid uniformity, the country seemed to delight in variety and a certain degree of randomness—with the Reformation simply adding a fur-ther, religious layer to the prevailing profusion. When late in history (in 1870), the country became a unified state, it did so with the zeal of the latecomer seeking to make up for lost time with fervent nationalistic and xenophobic virulence. As we know, national unity in the end was purchased with the blood of millions of victims.

Proust's words have a bearing on my life also in another sense. If I limit myself (for the moment) to German thinkers, my life has always stood under the aegis of two philosophical giants: Herder and Kant—the former the de-voted student of languages and cultural differences, the latter the philosopher of "reason" in the sense of "universal reason." The first was fond of travel-ing, of exploring distant lands and the different languages and customs of peoples. For this purpose, he engaged in multiple conversations or dialogues with representatives of different cultures and perspectives.[1] On the other hand, Kant remained ensconced in his native city all his life, shunning the discomfort of peregrination. In a way, the philosopher of Koenigsberg was an embodiment of the Cartesian *ego cogito*, a relentless explorer of the structure and inner dimensions of the mind (universally construed). The contrast, to be sure, should not be overdrawn. Herder did not just delight in cultural difference for its own sake. Rather, exploring different cultures and languages for him was part of a basic learning process, a process able to discern shared human possibilities across cultures. In this sense, Herder hoped for a general "uplifting to humaneness" (*Emporbildung zur Humanität*). For his part, Kant also did not refrain from commenting on human history and on the (good or bad) customs of different peoples. Moreover, as he always insisted, some measure of commonality seems to be required for every comparative inquiry.

Returning to my early background, I want to mention a formative experience that fitted both my Herderian and Kantian leanings. For the generations of my parents and grandparents, hostility between Germany and France was a basic fact of life, evident in a series of wars since 1870. For me—then a teenager—the end of World War II brought an unexpected surprise: the encounter and rapid reconciliation between French and German peoples. Having been liberated from the hateful xenophobia of the Nazi regime, young Germans watched with enthusiasm French cinema (the movies of René Clair, Marcel Carné, and Jean Renoir), inhaled the existentialist teachings of Jean-Paul Sartre and Albert Camus, and imbibed the poetry of Paul Valéry. In my own case, the enthusiasm had a strong philosophical component. I had learned that French philosopher Paul Ricoeur, while in a German POW camp, proceeded to study German philosophy, especially the German founders of phenomenology. In my view, this was surely an inspiring signal showing that a different path, away from hatred, was possible between countries and cultures.

As it happened, phenomenology soon became for me also the preferred philosophical perspective. As I quickly discovered, there are different ways of pursuing this perspective. In very broad terms, it seems possible to distinguish a Herderian from a quasi-Kantian approach: with the latter being manifest in Husserl's transcendental phenomenology (aiming to discern the "essence" of phenomena) and the former being intimated in Heidegger's hermeneutical version (accentuating the more concrete human situatedness or "being-in-the-world"). A similar divergence, I found, was also present in French existential phenomenology at the time. While Sartre's stress on radical freedom still paid tribute to the worldless Cartesian *cogito*, Merleau-Ponty's concern with "embodiment" brought to the fore the "difference" of worldly conditions and cultural contexts—while also disclosing more recessed differences between "the visible and the invisible" or between immanence and transcendence. Wrestling with these divergent approaches, I realized that I could not for long maintain a position of neutrality (figuratively between Herder and Kant) but had to forge my own path. Worldly experiences here came to my aid. Faced with the omni-presence of hegemonic powers in the world, I was less afraid of cultural relativism than of an overbearing global universalism trampling down on local traditions. A different manner of holding relativism at bay had to be discovered. I found it (eventually) in dialogue and "lateral" engagement.

The issue of universalism and difference continued to preoccupy me for several decades. After having completed my studies in Germany, I emigrated in the mid-1950s to America with the aim of pursuing there a career in political philosophy. I first went for a master's degree to Southern Illinois University, which then was emerging as center of John Dewey studies.[2] For my doctoral degree I went to Duke University, which, at that time, offered beautifully balanced programs both in philosophy and comparative politics. Not long after beginning my career, a dispute or debate erupted in the 1960s between two leading German thinkers: Jürgen Habermas and Hans-Georg Gadamer. At that point, Gadamer defended what he called a "universal hermeneutics," meaning that language and interpretation operate crucially in all fields of inquiry. While acknowledging the role of hermeneutics in the humanities, Habermas at the time sought to exclude it from the fields of empirical science and (his version of) critical theory, thereby clinging in some fashion to the Cartesian-Kantian idea of "apodictic" knowledge. Observing and participating in the debate, I was steadily drawn into the Gadamerian camp for strictly philosophical reasons. For how can language and hermeneutics be prevented from intruding into any domain? And how can dialogue and communication be restricted to the redemption of "rational validity claims"? The tension between reason and dialogue here asserts itself.

As one can see, my intellectual path was not smooth but punctured by debates: first the debate about the meaning of existentialism, and then the debate about language and hermeneutics. What I want to retain from these episodes is mainly one point: my siding in favor of difference and hermeneutics never amounted to a slide into a shallow pragmatism or relativism (which separated me later from some of the more exuberant forms of postmodernism). In the case of Gadamer, this slide is prevented by his moorings in Aristotle as well as in Herder/Hegel and in Heidegger. There is another point worth mentioning: my intellectual encounters up to this point were confined to European or Western philosophy. Despite my fondness for difference, my outlook was still basically Eurocentric or Western-centric. Although having been prepared by various episodes, the crucial step had not yet been made. This step happened in 1984 with my first visit to India. The occasion was a conference on political theory/philosophy at the University of Baroda in Gujarat. The convener, Bhikhu Parekh (himself an eminent political thinker), had invited a number of colleagues from Europe and America and also a large contingent of Indian scholars. Although in traveling to India I had expected a routine event, nothing routine-like occurred. I finally broke through my Western shell and, then and there, vowed to myself to become a serious intercultural scholar.

The Baroda conference was only a first step to be followed by many others. Having met and established good relations with many Indian colleagues, I was invited subsequently to numerous universities, bringing me back to India once or twice every year. My chief intellectual concern in India was basically cultural-historical: how to relate the older traditions (from the *Upanishads* to the great philosophical schools) to the renaissance or renewal of India during the last two centuries? To gain access to the older traditions, I began to study the classical language (Sanskrit); in the period of renewal, my interest focused mainly on the thought of Gandhi and his contemporaries. Aided by some good teachers (and a dictionary), my language study enabled me eventually to savor the *Bhagavad Gita* in the original. My Gandhi studies yielded invitations to many Gandhi circles and institutes throughout the country.

The breaking of my Eurocentric shell in 1984 was reflected in several of my subsequent publications. Together with an Indian colleague, Ganesh Devy, I collected materials for a volume offering a broad overview of intellectual trends and perspectives in India during the past hundred years (the volume was ultimately published by SAGE India under the title *Between Tradition and Modernity: India's Search for Identity*). In 1986 I was invited to a major conference in Delhi on the thought of the leading Indian philosopher (and second president of the republic) Sarvepalli Radhakrishnan; my contribution titled "On Being and Existence: A Western View" appeared in the *Centenary Volume* of 1989. In the same year my book *Margins of Political Discourse* appeared with a central chapter titled "Gandhi as Mediator between East and West." As I tried to show, Gandhi occupies a particularly significant role in our time: as a mediator between different cultures but also between tradition and modernity, past and future. Frequent trips brought me north to Delhi where I became a steady participant in the activities of the Center for the Study of Developing Societies (CSDS), headed by Rajni Kothari and Ashis Nandy. Several of my published papers deal with that Center and its members.

In 1991, I was awarded a Fulbright Research Grant, which enabled me to spend a full year in India. That year was very important to me; it enabled me to live up more fully to my vow. Pursuing my major research agenda (the linkage of traditional and modern India), I visited again numerous universities and research centers all over the subcontinent. As could not be otherwise, my intercultural commitment penetrated steadily more deeply into my publications. Taking a leaf from Edward Said, I published in 1996 the book *Beyond Orientalism: Essays on Cross-Cultural Encounter*, containing such chapters as "Heidegger, Bhakti, and Vedanta" and "Western Thought and Indian Thought." This was followed in 1998 by my book *Alternative Visions:*

Paths in the Global Village. During these years, the thought grew in me of the desirability of launching a new field of academic study that would bridge the fields of philosophy, politics, and the social sciences and that might be called comparative political theory/philosophy. In 1997 I edited with a colleague a special issue of *The Review of Politics* called "Non-Western Political Thought." Two years later I edited a volume titled *Border Crossings: Toward a Comparative Political Theory.* This volume became the launching pad of a new book series published by Lexington Books titled "Global Encounters: Studies in Comparative Political Theory."

As I should add, in the spirit of my intercultural vow, India for me was not only a place of arrival but also of departure for new inquiries. During my stays in India I also met many Buddhists and Muslims, and I made it part of my commitment to explore these spiritual paths as well. During the decades following my year in India, I was able to spend considerable time in China, Korea, and Japan, mainly at universities and conferences. Always on the look-out for the connection between the old and the new, tradition and modernity, I focused there especially on the living impact of Buddhism and Confucianism on contemporary social and political developments. In China I was fortunate to be invited to several major conferences on the revival of Confucian or neo-Confucian teachings—finding my understanding enhanced by the helpful friendship of Tu Weiming and other experts. In both China and Korea my focus was also on the relevance of traditional religious beliefs for present-day democratic initiatives. In Japan my main preoccupation was with the Zen Buddhism of the Kyoto School, chiefly Nishida and Nishitani, and its relation to contemporary Japanese life. My writings published in the new century frequently refer to these names and topics.[3]

I do not wish to transform this account into a travelogue, which would not be instructive. There is, however, one aspect I cannot forget to mention, especially in light of current global developments. This is my engagement with the Islamic world. Here, my intercultural zeal led me to a number of countries: Morocco, Egypt, Turkey, Iran, and Malaysia. As always, my concern was with the philosophical understanding of the relation between past and present, especially between classical Islamic thought and present aspirations and possibilities. In Morocco, I visited repeatedly with philosopher Abed al-Jabri who insisted strongly on the need for Arab-Islamic "renewal" to meet the challenges of today. In Egypt, a similar message—perhaps in more radical terms—was conveyed to me by philosopher Hassan Hanafi. In Turkey, I had the pleasure of befriending Professor Ahmet Davutoglu (before he became prime minister), a humanist firmly committed to the "dialogue of civilizations." In Iran, I encountered a similar commitment in philosopher Abdolkarim Soroush and in the group of scholars loosely associated with Ayatollah Khatami. In Malaysia, I have enjoyed the friendship of the president of Just World Trust, Chandra Musaffar, a man fervently devoted to the pursuit justice everywhere in the world.

One of the lessons I learned in my Islamic encounters is the entirely negotiable character of the so-called "Sunni-Shia" divide (a difference pushed into bloody conflict today by some leading global powers). In general terms, the preference for dialogue and mutual understanding was present in all my intercultural studies—starting with the German-French encounter in my youth. My forays into different cultures and religions were never prompted by idle touristic curiosity nor by scholastic pedantry, but by a practical impulse: to find out how—coming from very diverse backgrounds—people can yet live peacefully and justly in this world. *Opus justitiae pax.*

NOTES

1. Compare on this point my "Truth and Difference: Some Lessons from Herder," in *Alternative Visions: Paths in the Global Village* (Lanham, MD: Rowman & Littlefield, 1998).

2. In my understanding, John Dewey was the primary American philosopher of democracy. I only learned later that Dewey was increasingly sidelined in America by the rise of neoconservatism.

3. Among my publications I want to mention only a few: *Dialogue Among Civilizations: Some Exemplary Voices* (2002; dedicated to Gadamer who passed away that year); *Peace Talks—Who Will Listen* (2004); *In Search of the Good Life* (2007); *Integral Pluralism: Beyond Culture Wars* (2010); *Being in the World: Dialogue and Cosmopolis* (2013); and, with Zhao Tingyang, *Contemporary Chinese Political Thought* (2012). In terms of professional and semi-professional engagements, I served in 2004–2005 as president of the Society for Asian and Comparative Philosophy (SACP); and in 2005–2015 as co-chair of the international NGO World Public Forum—Dialogue of Civilization (headquartered in Vienna and meeting every fall in Rhodes, Greece).

Appendix C

Interview:
Joseph Camilleri with Fred Dallmayr [1]

Camilleri: You have over many years explored the contemporary human predicament that centres on our seeming inability to manage let alone celebrate difference—difference understood as the plurality of cultures, religions, nationalities, ethnicities, states, political systems and ideologies, and, of course the differential access to wealth and resources. Your latest book *Being in the World: Dialogue and Cosmopolis* (University of Kentucky Press, 2013) broaches the subject by exploring the notion of cosmopolis and cosmopolitanism. We have had several contributions to this perspective in recent years. What are the defining characteristics of the cosmopolitanism you have in mind?

Dallmayr: The notion of "cosmopolitanism" has of late gained prominence because of its potential ability to chart a path beyond an abstract, undifferentiated universalism and an array of self-enclosed particular identities (where the latter can refer to cultural, religious, ethnic, political and/or economic identities). In contemporary literature, the term is used in many different ways. In my book, *Being in the World*, I distinguish between three modalities: an empirical, a normative, and a practical or interactive type. The empirical type coincides basically with the notion of "globalization" and involves the factual extension of economic markets, technological advances, and digital information processes around the globe. Arjun Appadurai has called it "cellular globalization" because of its diffuse and amorphous character. The normative type refers to the moral and legal rules which govern or should govern the relations between different identities; of crucial importance here are the universal principles established by the Western Enlightenment and by modern international law. The practical type—to which I give primacy in my book—places the emphasis on the lateral interactions and mutual engagement between particular identities in our world. Taken by itself, empirical globalization can lead, and has led, to enormous social and economic inequalities and systems of global exploitation and domination. These ills are to be corrected or at least mitigated by the universal principles of normative cosmopolitanism. In my view, however, these principles so far are not sufficiently anchored in practical conduct, a conduct which has to be cultivated and fostered on the level of concrete multilateral experiences and engagements, preferably through interactive dialogue.

C: Would you agree that all strands of cosmopolitan thought are to a greater or lesser extent subject to an unresolved tension, namely the tension between abstract universal ethical principles and concrete cultural contexts? If so, is this tension resolvable?

D: There is a basic tension inherent in philosophy as such, but also in cosmopolitan thought. This is the tension between the abstract and the concrete, between universalism and particularism, or (in an older formulation) between "the one" and "the many." Since this tension is endemic to human thinking, it cannot be removed, but it can be mitigated and tempered. The most promising tempering factor is practice, practical conduct, and especially interactive dialogue. The classical source of this approach is Aristotle's ethics which moves between Platonic absolutism and Sophistic relativism and which centerstages the practice of virtues. In several of my writings I have pursued this middle path: especially in my *In Search of the Good Life* (2007), in *Integral Pluralism: Beyond Culture Wars* (2010), and most recently in *Being in the World*. In charting this path, I have differentiated myself from utilitarianism (anchored in self-interest) and also from versions of Kantianism or neo-Kantianism (exemplified by John Rawls and Habermasian "discourse ethics") which I have found to be too abstract and too aloof from practical engagement.

C: If we are to argue, as you do both in your latest book and in earlier writings, that dialogue offers a way forward in reconciling the unity of the human family with the plurality of its tribes, how should we visualise this dialogue—its processes, its participants and its potential outcomes?

D: As a mode of practical interaction, I find dialogue indeed a crucial element in the effort to reconcile unity and plurality. The emphasis on dialogue can be traced back to Aristotelian *phronesis*; to Hegel's stress on mutual "recognition," to Gadamerian hermeneutics (who relies strongly on both Aristotle and Hegel) and to Heidegger's notions of *Mitsein* (co-being) and "letting-be." Ideally, dialogue should involve all people who have a stake in an issue and its potential outcomes. It is important to realize, however, that dialogue does not only involve verbal exchanges—and certainly not only exchanges of rational "validity claims" (in the Habermasian sense). Construed as a sustained mutual engagement and learning process, dialogue can also proceed in the mode of gestures, glances, subtle cues, and even occasional silences. In this sense, dialogue forms part of what Merleau-Ponty called "inter-corporeality" (or embodied relationships). The result of dialogue is not necessarily a consensus or "fusion of horizons," but can also take the form of a better grasp of mutual differences and sometimes a postponement of further negotiations.

C: Would you say that cosmopolitan ideas are derived primarily from Western intellectual traditions, or can they be said to have equally important roots in non-Western civilizations?

D: In my view, modern cosmopolitan ideas are largely derived from Western intellectual traditions—but not exclusively so. A major problem is that cosmopolitanism, as advanced by Western traditions, is often closely linked with imperialism or the striving for global domination—and also with (what Edward Said called) "Orientalism," that is, attempts to define non-Western cultures exclusively in Western categories or conceptual frameworks. This linkage puts a stain on cosmopolitanism and sometimes delegitimizes it in non-Western eyes. Hence, a great effort is needed in the West to cleanse cosmopolitanism of traces of imperialism and unilateral hegemony. This effort is likely to be more promising of success if it can find parallels in non-Western traditions. Such traces can be found in the classical Indian notion of the universal "*brahman*," in Confucian ideas of "humaneness" (*jen*) and more generally in the Asian emphasis on the "way" (*tao*).

C: Is the cosmopolitan dialogue you have in mind amenable to concrete, constructive engagement in the here and now?

D: Since the cosmopolitan dialogue I have in mind arises from concrete mutual engagement, it should also be able to feed back into concrete global interactions. To be sure, dialogue is not the same as direct political intervention. However, dialogue can contribute to the clarification of contested issues, to the reduction of prejudices and mutual animosities, and in this way can prepare the ground for a (hopefully) amicable settlement of conflicts. Dialogue—I want to emphasize—is not the same as idle chit-chat or empty chatter. Dialogue has an ethical orientation or purpose: to contribute to a just or fair resolution of disputes.

C: In several of your writings you have suggested that "in modern times nature has tended to be marginalized, colonized and abused." How is the exile of nature as the dominant strand in modern western thought to be explained?

D: The fact that "nature" in modern times has been marginalized, colonized or exiled derives from the dominant modern intellectual paradigm: the dichotomy between mind and matter, between subject and object, between the *cogito* inside and the world outside. This dichotomy was most famously formulated by René Descartes. Based on this dualism, modern science—inaugurated by Francis Bacon—proceeded to transform nature into an external object, into a target to be analyzed and controlled by human mind or reason. In this paradigm, mind or reason functions as a sovereign ruler mastering the universe. Ultimately, of course, the dualism boomerangs against the master by alienating or exiling humanity from its own "nature" or natural grounding.

C: Is it possible to recover a different and healthier understanding of the relationship with nature? How might a dialogue between Western and non-Western traditions assist us in this difficult enterprise?

D: One of the major endeavors in our time is to recover a non-dualistic and more harmonious relation between humanity and nature. My book *Return to Nature?* (2012) points in this direction. The task is to find a common ground which does not simply collapse or wipe out relevant distinctions in an amorphous "naturalism." In my book, I argue in favor of a differentiated wholeness or holism, a wholeness which neither smothers distinctions in a totalizing oneness nor separates or divorces them from each other. Such an outlook can find considerable support in Asian traditions of thought, especially in the Upanishadic notion of "*brahman*," the Indian philosophy of "Advaita Vedanta," and in East Asian reflections on the "way" (*tao*) which is neither inside nor outside, neither purely mental nor purely corporeal. Among more recent thinkers, I have been particularly influenced by Raimon Panikkar's triadic or trinitarian correlation of the divine, humanity, and nature (the so-called "cosmotheandric" relation).

C: Do you wish to add some further comments?

D: Yes, an issue which I regard as crucial both in the contemporary context and in the emerging context of cosmopolis is the conflict between "freedom" and "solidarity." Ultimately, this conflict or dualism also goes back to the Cartesian dichotomy between mind and matter, inside and outside. Deriving from this dichotomy, the modern mind (in the West) has tended to assert its complete independence or "freedom" from the external world, including the world of inter-human or societal relations and obligations. Human freedom in Western modernity has tended to be construed chiefly as a freedom "from" external entanglements (often called "negative freedom"); to the extent that it is given an active or "positive" meaning, freedom involves tendentially the imposition of the "subject's" mind or will on the outer world in the form of a project, blueprint or ideology. The term "subject" here can mean an individual subject, but also a group subject or even national subject (provided its project is seen as a unilateral and monological trajectory).

The dualism of freedom and solidarity has played itself out in both domestic and global contexts. During the last two centuries, the conflict assumed massive, even monumental proportions, in the sense that the Western world has styled itself as the "Free World," while the "Eastern" world has come to be seen as inhibited by "unfreedom" in the form of socialism, communion, despotism, and totalitarianism. In the West, the term "solidarity" has acquired a pejorative connotation due to its frequent association with socialism and communism. This pejorative meaning is particularly prominent in the economic domain where laissez-faire capitalism and neo-liberalism are celebrated regardless of their consequences in terms of social inequality, widespread misery, and the destruction of any meaningful solidarity. The zenith of cut-throat economic freedom was reached in the financial meltdown of 2008–09 with its devastating effects on social and public life.

Despite its disastrous effects, the lessons of the meltdown have not been learned. To make things worse, geopolitical rivalries have reinvigorated the legacy of the Cold War—with the result that it has become customary to speak of Cold War II. With some modifications, the actors in the new geopolitical scenario resemble those of the past. On the one side, there is again the "Free World" comprising mainly North America and the NATO countries. On the other side, we find Russia, China, and to a lesser extent some BRICS countries. (The situation in the Muslim world is presently so confused and chaotic that nobody can predict the outcome. Only one thing is clear: tendencies toward "theocracy" are not readily compatible with the image of the "Free World"). Given the ongoing militarization and partial nuclearization of geopolitics, fears are not unfounded that Cold War II may lead to a "nuclear winter."

I have just finished writing a book called *Freedom and Solidarity: Toward New Beginnings.* [In the meantime, the text has been published by University of Kentucky Press, 2016]. The book seeks to go to the philosophical root of the dichotomy between freedom and social responsibility. To overcome the dichotomy, the book pleads for a new conception or redefinition of the key terms "freedom" and "solidarity," in such a way that the two terms are no longer seen as antitheses but as mutually complementary and even mutually constitutive. As should be evident, the book seeks not only to effect a conceptual realignment but (more importantly) a social-political and geopolitical realignment, thus making a contribution to global peace with justice.

NOTE

1. At the time of the interview (2015), Joseph Camilleri was a senior professor in international politics and peace studies at La Trobe University in Melbourne, Australia. For other interviews see Fred Dallmayr with Ghoncheh Tazmini, "Genuine Dialogue Requires Not Only Talking but a Great Deal of Listening," in Piotr Dutkiewicz and Richard Sakwa, eds., *22 Ideas to Fix the World: Conversations with the World's Foremost Thinkers* (New York: New York University Press, 2013), pp. 286–301; and Farah Godrej, "An Interview with Fred Dallmayr," in Godrej, ed., *Fred Dallmayr: Critical Phenomenology, Cross-Cultural Theory, and Cosmopolitanism* (New York: Routledge, 2017), pp. 250–261.

Index

Abe, Masao, 67
Abu Zayd, Nasr, 66
aging, 2–3
al-Jabri, Muhammad, 66
American Political Science Association, 56
American revolution, 25–26
Ames, Roger, 66
Anawati, Georges, 66
Arab Spring, 77–78
Arendt, Hannah, 71, 78, 85
Ashcraft, Richard, 57
Augsburg, 4; architecture, 4–5;
    firebombing of, 6–7, 10; Fritz
    Reisinger, 9; Great Depression, 6–7;
    history, 4–6; religion, 6, 7, 9, 10; St.
    Anna school, 9–11; St. Stephan school,
    9–11; St. Ulrich churches, 5;
    synagogue, 13; World War II, 6–7, 9
Avineri, Shlomo, 62

Balzer, Ilse, 21–22, 22–23
Banares Hindu University, 60
behavioralism. See empiricism
Bell, Daniel A., 81
Benhabib, Seyla, 56
Benjamin, Walter, 71
Bentham, Jeremy, 53
Bernasconi, Robert, ix
Bernhard, Berl, 46
Bernhardt, Robert, 12
Bernstein, Richard, 56, 64

Berry, Thomas, 77
Bhargava, Rajeev, 57
Bobbio, Norberto, 2–3, 18–20
Bruns, Gerald, 55
Brussels, 16
Buddhism. See Japanese Buddhism
Butler, Judith, 56
Butterworth, Charles, 67
Buttigieg, Joseph, 55

Cabral, Amilcar, 70
Camilleri, Joseph, 119–124
Camus, Albert, 85
cancer, 86
capitalism, 78–79, 83
Caputo, John, 28
career. See academic career
Centre for the Study of Developing
    Societies (CSDS), 65
Chatterjee, Partha, 57
childhood, 4–13
China, 79–81; travel to, 79–80
Cicero, 2
civil rights movement, 25, 26, 46
Cold War, 34, 36, 65; revival of Cold War
    mentality after September 11, 68–69,
    78; opposition to Cold War mentality,
    70–71
comparative political theory, development
    of field, 67
Confucianism, 79–81

Connolly, William, 35–36, 56
cosmopolitanism, 82–83

D'Sa, Francis, 59–60
Dahrendorf, Ralf, 31
Dasilva, Fabio, 55
Davutoglu, Ahmet, 66
de Bary, William Theodore, 76
democracy, 70–71; contradiction of self-rule and hegemony, 75; ethical democracy, 72–75; democratic movements after 2008, 75–76
De Nobile College, 59–60
Derrida, Jacques: lectures on Nietzsche, 54–55; meeting in Paris, 49–52; philosophical influence, 52
De Smet, Richard, 59–60
death, 4
Deleuze, Gilles, 53
Demenchonok, Edward, 87
Denmark, 77
Deutsch, Eliot, 66
Dewey, John, 21, 85
Duke University, 23–26; choice of academia, 22; choice of America, 22

East-West Center (University of Hawaii), 66
education: doctorate, 16–17; legal studies, 14–17; primary and secondary, 8–11. *See also* political philosophy
Egypt, 66
empiricism, 24, 30
equality, concepts of, 25–26; Montesquieu, 25–26; doctoral dissertation, 25–26
Erasmus, 20, 71
ethical democracy. *See* democracy, ethical
Euben, Roxanne, 76
Eurocentrism. *See* multiculturalism
European Society of Culture, 19
European unification, 19–20
exchange theory, 31

family, 7–8; brother Albert, 10; brother Horst, 10; marriage, 23; parents, 7–8; wife Ilse, 21–22, 22–23; children, 28
Flynn, Bernard, 103–112
Foucault, Michel: meeting in Paris, 50–52; and Nietzsche, 52; panopticon, 52;

philosophical influence, 52–53
Francis (pope), as pathfinder, 87
Frankfurt School, 30, 32, 45
Free University (Brussels), 16
freedom, concepts of, 34, 36
freedom, 34, 36; need to pair with solidarity, 85
French revolution, 25–26

Gadamer, Hans-Georg, 36–37, 38–39; conflict with Habermas, 41–42, 53; seminar on Martin Heidegger, 39–40; support of Heidegger, 43
Gandhi, Mohandas, 59, 62, 71; and ethical self-rule (swaraj), 75; work of synthesis, 65
Gehlen, Arnold, 31–32
globalism. *See* multiculturalism
Goethe, Johann, 71
the "good life", 73–74; as pedagogy, 74. *See also* democracy, ethical
group-based theory, 31
Guardini, Romano, 15
Gujarati, 59

Habermas, Jürgen, 36–38; conflict with Gadamer, 41–42, 53; limitations of, 62; and postmodernism, 52
Halbfass, Wilhelm, 60
Hamburg, 36–37, 40. *See also* University of Hamburg
Hampshire, Stuart, 48
Hanafi, Hassan, 66
Hayek, Friedrich, 30
Hegel, Georg, 35, 56, 62, 64
hegemony. *See* democracy, ethical
Heidegger, Martin, 27–28, 43–45, 49, 64; being-in-the-world, 82; and Frankfurt School, 62; and freedom, 83–85; and Nazism, 43, 45, 63; *The Other Heidegger* (1993), 63; sheltering of the divine, 71
Heller, Agnes, 64
Herder, Johann Gottfried, 70
Hesburgh, Theodore M., 46; retirement, 70
Husserl, Edmund, 32

Ibn Rushd (Averroes), 71

India, 56–61; Fulbright grant in, 59;
    darshanas, 59; diversity of, 65
Institute of European Studies, 17, 22
International Studies Association (ISA), 72
Intercultural studies, 113–118
Iran, 78
Iraq War, 71
Islam, 65; American tendencies after
    September 11, 68, 77
Istanbul, 66

Japanese Buddhism, 67
Jñanadev, 74
Jung, Hwa Yol, 28, 67

Kant, Immanuel, 73
Kar, Prafulla, 59
Kateb, George, 56
Kaviraj, Sudipta, 57
Kisiel, Theodore, 28
Kothari, Rajni, 65, 70
Kroc Institute for International Peace
    Studies (University of Notre Dame), 72
Kunstmann, Josef, 12
Kyoto School. *See* Japanese Buddhism

Lacan, Jacques, 53
Lang, Gregor, 11, 12
Larson, Gerald, 66
Lasswell, Harold, 31
Lefort, Claude, 53
Leibniz, Gottfried, 74
liberalism, 34, 36; definitions of, 35
Libya, 78
Loyola University (Chicago), 54
Lukes, Steven, ix, 48

MacIntyre, Alasdair, 73
Madras Christian College, 61
Madras University, 61
Marcel, Gabriel, 2
marriage. *See* family
McBride, William, 56
McCarthy, Thomas, 32–33, 56
Mehta, J. L., 60
Mehta, V. R., 57
Menzel, Adolf, 13
Merleau-Ponty, Maurice, 28, 30, 36
Merton, Thomas, as pathfinder, 87

Middle East, 78, 86
military intervention, 78
Milwaukee Downer College, 26
Minogue, Kenneth, 57
Mishkin, Adam, 13
Montesquieu, 25–26, 74
Morocco, 66, 76
Moscow, 76
multiculturalism: and field of comparative
    philosophy, 66; and field of
    intercultural studies, 113–118; among
    Indian scholars, 57; practice vs. theory,
    57–59; Western tradition's support of,
    64. *See also* cosmopolitanism
Munich, 14–16
music: in India, 57; at Oxford, 46; playing
    piano, 13
Muzaffar, Chandra, 70

Nandy, Ashis, 57, 65, 70
Nazism: Heidegger and, 43, 45, 63;
    resistance to, 85
Nawiasky, Hans, 16
neoconservatism, 36
Nepal, 60
New School for Social Research, 63
Nietzsche, Friedrich, 20, 49, 52; graduate
    seminar on, 54
Nikolaus of Cusa, 74
Nishida, Kitaro, 67
Nishitani, Keiji, 67
Nussbaum, Martha, 83

Oakeshott, Michael, 30
Ortega y Gasset, José, 15
Oxford, 46–53
Oxford University, 46; philosophical
    trends at, 48

Panikkar, Raimon, 66, 71, 77, 85; as
    pathfinder, 87; *The Rhythm of Being*, 83
Pantham, Thomas, 57
Parekh, Bhikhu, 56, 67
Parel, Anthony, 67, 76
Paris, 48–53
Paul, Julius, 21
peace studies, 71
Peinim Ni, 81

philosophy: comparative philosophy, 66; comparative political theory, development of field, 67; Continental, 55; ethical life, 62; Heidegger vs. Frankfurt School, 62; humanity/nature split, 77; Indian philosophy, 56–61; intercultural studies, 113–118; mind/ matter split, 77; *See also individual theories;* multiculturalism; political philosophy

Plessner, Helmuth, 31–32

political philosophy: development at Purdue, 30; doctoral dissertation, 25–26; doctorate studies at Duke University, 24, 24–25; graduate studies at Southern Illinois University, 21; graduate studies at Turin, 18–20; humanistic approach, 24–25, 30; "images of man", 31; vs. political theory, 33; "two cultures", 30–31; undergraduate studies, 14–15. *See also* equality; freedom; *individual theories*

positivism. *See* empiricism

postmodernism, 37, 48–49

poststructuralism. *See* postmodernism

pragmatism, 21, 24

Proust, Marcel, 1

Psathas, George, 28

publications: *Achieving Our World: Toward a Global and Plural Democracy* (2001), 70; *Against Apocalypse: Holding the World Together* (2016), 87; *Alternative Visions: Paths in the Global Village* (1998), 70; *Being in the World: Dialogue and Cosmopolis* (2013), 83, 119–124; *Beyond (Neo-)Liberalism: Toward a Social and Democratic Commonwealth*, 87; *The Communicative Ethics Controversy*, 37; *Contemporary Chinese Political Thought: Perspectives and Debates* (2012), 81; *Critical Encounters* (1987), 61; *Democracy to Come: Politics as Relational Praxis* (2017), 87; *Dialogue Among Civilizations: Some Exemplary Voices* (2002), 70–71; *Freedom and Emergency Power in the Cold War*, 25; *Freedom and Solidarity: Toward New*

Beginnings (2015), 87; Global Encounters: Studies in Comparative Political Theory book series, 67; *Integral Pluralism: Beyond Culture Wars* (2010), 76; *Margins of Political Discourse* (1989), 61; *Materialienband zu Erkenntnis und Interesse*, 37; *Mindfulness and Letting Be: On Engaged Thinking and Acting* (2014), 87; *Peace Talks—Who Will Listen?* (2004), 71; "Political Science and the Two Cultures", 30; *Return to Nature? An Ecological Counterhistory* (2011), 77; *In Search of the Good Life* (2007), 74, 103–112; *Small Wonder: Global Power and Its Discontents* (2005), 71–72; *Spiritual Guides: Pathfinders in the Desert* (2017), 87; *Twilight of Subjectivity*, 45; *Understanding and Social Inquiry*, 32–33; *A World Beyond Global Disorder: The Courage to Hope*, 87

Purdue University, 26–30

Rajan, Sundara, 60

Rankin, Robert, 25, 46

Rasmussen, David, 56, 103–112

rational choice theory, 31

religion: in Augsburg, 6, 7, 9; loving without knowing, 73; regnum tuum, 86

Richardson, William, 28

Ricoeur, Paul, 4, 53

Rolin, Henri, 16

Rorty, Richard, 52

Rosemont, Henry, Jr., 66

Rothacker, Erich, 31

Roy, Arundhati, 71

Russian Federation, 78, 86

Said, Edward, 52

Sallis, John, 28

Sanskrit, 59

Scheler, Max, 30, 31

Schiller, Friedrich, 74

Schmitt, Carl, 15

Schnabel, Franz, 15

Schoolman, Morton, 56

Schrag, Calvin, 27–28, 56

Schürmann, Reiner, 64

Schutz, Alfred, 32
Seoul, 76
September 11 attacks, 68–70; effect on
    American policy, 68, 77; memories of
    World War II, 69
Shapiro, Michael, 56
Snow, Lord, 30
Society for Asian and Comparative
    Philosophy, 66
Society for Phenomenology and Existential
    Philosophy (SPEP), 28, 56, 66
Society for Phenomenology and the
    Human Sciences (SPHS), 28
solidarity, 85
Soroush, Abdulkarim, 66, 71
Southern Illinois University, 20–21
St. Bonaventure, 74
Stepaniants, Marietta, 66
Strauss, Leo, 34–35
structural-functionalist theory, 31
systems theory, 31

Tanabe, Haime, 67
Taylor, Charles, 48, 62, 67; and
    postmodernism, 52; *A Secular Age*, 83
terrorism, 68, 86
Thoreau, Henry David, 85
Tillich, Paul, 27–28; as pathfinder, 87;
    support of Heidegger, 43
Tu Weiming, 66, 81
Turin, 17–20, 22

U.S. Civil Rights Commission, 46
Ulm, 4
Understanding and Social Inquiry, 32–33
UNESCO, 72
UNESCO, 76
University of Aarhus, 77
University of Baroda, 56–59; Fulbright
    grant in, 59

University of Cairo, 66
University of Hamburg, 63
University of Hawaii, 66
University of Notre Dame, 46, 54–55;
    teaching and students, 55;
    interdisciplinary appointment, 61; after
    September 11, 70; retirement from, 72
University of Rabat, 66

Vattanky, John, 59–60
Vattimo, Gianni, 71
violence. *See* military intervention
virtue ethics, 73; disappearance from
    political discourse, 76
Voegelin, Eric, 30, 34–35

Waldenfels, Bernhard, 56, 63
war, attitudes toward, 10, 78; foreign
    intervention, 78; global war, 68–69;
    Pindar, 10
Watson, Stephen, 55
Weber, Max, 32
Westphal, Merold, 28
White, Stephen, 56
Wilson, Robert, 24
Winch, Peter, 30
Wolin, Sheldon, 35
work, during youth, 13, 14
World Congress of Philosophy, 76
World Days of Philosophy, 76
World Public Forum—Dialogue of
    Civilizations, 78–79, 87
World War II, 9–10, 13, 86
Wrinn, Stephen, 67

Young, Iris Marion, 56
Yusa, Michiko, 67

Zhao Tingyang, 81–82